PLAN A LIFE YOU LOVE

& LIVE IT OUT LOUD NOW

*The Bold Sequel to the Book
That Changed Lives*

HANNA OLIVAS

ALONG WITH 6 INSPIRING AUTHORS

ISBN: 978-1-966798-86-6

TABLE OF CONTENTS

INTRODUCTION...4

My Pain Turned Into My Plan
  By Hanna Olivas.. 6

From Shattered Dreams to the Courage to Begin Again:
A Journey of Resilience
  By Gabby Gutierrez...21

Windows into My Soul
  By Carmen Maendel 28

Dare to Dream Again!
  By Kali Morris... 43

A True Story of Healing, Hope, and a Faith-Led Reset
After Long COVID
  By Erica Elliott... 55

FLIP Waiting to Creating: The Quantum Practice of Gratitude
  By Sylvia Becker-Hill..70

Drift or Drive: Cancel Autopilot and Design a Life on Purpose
  By Cyndee Paulson-Heer...88

INTRODUCTION

by Hanna Olivas

Welcome to *Plan A Life You Love & Live It Out Loud Now*: *The Bold Sequel to the Book that Changed Lives,* a sacred space where truth is told, dreams are reclaimed, and courage is called forth.

This isn't just another feel-good read. It's a call to action: a soul-level invitation to pause, reflect, and realign. The book is filled with the lived experiences of women who decided enough was enough, women who stopped shrinking, stopped settling, and dared to imagine more. They didn't wait for perfect timing, external validation, or permission. They chose to show up fully, flaws and all, and design a life that felt like home.

The book itself is part memoir and part rally cry. The Companion Journal, *Plan A Life You Love & Live It Out Loud Now Journal*: *A Bold Continuation of the Journey that Transformed Lives,* extends that message by giving you the space to process, reflect, and act on what you're learning. Inside, you'll find reflective prompts, guided exercises, and practical tools designed to move you from insight to action. Together, the book and Journal become a powerful duo: one inspires, the other equips.

You don't have to have it all figured out to begin. You just have to be willing to begin.

So wherever you are in your journey (dreaming, healing, or rebuilding) this book and Journal are for you. Let them remind you that your voice matters, your desires matter, you matter.

This is your permission slip to stop waiting and start living.

Let's begin.

Hanna Olivas

Founder and CEO of SHE RISES STUDIOS

https://www.linkedin.com/company/she-rises-studios/
https://www.facebook.com/sherisesstudios
https://www.instagram.com/sherisesstudios_llc/
www.SheRisesStudios.com

Author, Speaker, and Founder. Hanna was born and raised in Las Vegas, Nevada, and has paved her way to becoming one of the most influential women of 2022. Hanna is the co-founder of She Rises Studios and the founder of the Brave & Beautiful Blood Cancer Foundation. Her journey started in 2017 when she was first diagnosed with Multiple Myeloma, an incurable blood cancer. Now more than ever, her focus is to empower other women to become leaders because The Future is Female. She is currently traveling and speaking publicly to women to educate them on entrepreneurship, leadership, and owning the female power within.

My Pain Turned Into My Plan

By Hanna Olivas

The Night the House Went Quiet

When my father left, the house didn't just get quieter. It changed color. I can still see his old jacket on the chair, the one that smelled like motor oil and cologne. I remember the click of the door, the way the air hung in the hallway as if the walls themselves were deciding whether to breathe. He didn't slam it. That almost made it worse. Slamming carries the promise of a return. Quiet feels permanent.

I learned then that goodbyes don't always announce themselves. Sometimes they just... leave.

The world kept moving, as if a truck hadn't just backed over my chest. Homework needed doing. Dishes needed washing. My mother worked and cried in the shower and pretended not to. My grandma cooked and prayed and whispered, "Mija, Dios te ve," as if the words could glue me together from the inside.

But something else happened. The silence taught me to listen to the tiny voice that said, "You're still here." And being here would become my rebellion.

When Innocence Was Stolen

I will say this plainly because a thousand other girls and women have a knot in their throats that won't unravel unless someone says it first: I was touched where I should have been safe. I was cornered in rooms meant for family and told to keep secrets that tasted like rust. I learned to count ceiling tiles to leave my body. I learned to smile with my mouth while my eyes left the room.

Abuse is a thief with a master key. It takes your sense of safety, your trust in the shape of people, and your ability to believe in your own body. It leaves fingerprints you spend years trying to scrub off in hot water that always runs cold too soon.

There is no pretty way to survive this. There is only learning that shame belongs to the one who did the breaking, never to the one they tried to break. It took me too long to know that. It might take you time, too. That's okay. Healing doesn't wear a stopwatch. But hear me: What happened to you is part of your story, not the author of it. You are the pen. Not the stain.

Mario

Grief has a sound. It's not the wail you imagine. It's the sound a room makes when it's holding back a scream. The monitor's beep. The hushed shuffle of nurses who run out of words. The doctor's voice trying to be both soft and clinical, missing the mark on both. The heartbeat you pray to hear, and the quiet that follows.

Eight and a half months. I knew the shape of his kicks. I knew the rhythm of him. I had names picked out on sticky notes and baby blankets folded with hope. And then the world fell through a trapdoor.

There are no metaphors that do justice to a mother's arms left empty. There are only facts: There was a baby. There was a womb, a heartbeat, and a future. Then there was a room full of equipment and a silence that rearranged my DNA.

I was furious at God. Not annoyed. Not confused. Furious. If faith is a muscle, anger is sometimes the weight you lift before you can lift anything else. I told Him I was done. Then I screamed. Then I slept on the tile. Then I got up because my other children still needed breakfast. Grief and duty can share a kitchen. It's cruel. It's also how some of us survive.

If you are reading this with an empty nursery and a heart you don't recognize, I won't preach at you. I will sit on the floor with you. I will tell you the truth: You will never "get over" it. You will carry him in a way that hurts less and honors more. Love doesn't stop. It changes shape. And on the days when breathing is a job, we will count the breaths together.

Bloodlines and Belonging

Half-Latina in a world that loves full boxes. My dad is gone. My last name is opening doors sometimes and closing them the other times. I learned to pronounce myself differently in different rooms. Too brown here, too light there. That's how identity fractures: not always by violence, sometimes by a thousand side-eye cuts.

My mother and grandma taught me culture with their hands. Food, prayer, and stories. I built my own bridge between bloodlines and stood in the middle, not to apologize, but to declare that I am whole. I wasn't designed to fit a box. I was built to break them. If you have spent a lifetime auditioning for rooms you already own, come home to yourself. Your skin, your tongue, and your history areall invitations. No explanations needed.

Weddings, Wars, and the Work of Love

No one warns you how loud the past can be inside a marriage. Two people say "I do," and a crowd of ghosts nods along. We had love, we had kids, and we had a blended map with more detours than directions. We also had nights so tense the air stung, arguments that left furniture untouched but left us shattered anyway, and paperwork that hovered like a storm we begged not to break.

Betrayal doesn't have to be a kiss in the wrong place. It can be a promise undone by a thousand weary choices. We came close to the cliff. We peeked over. We shook. Some nights I had a bag half-packed, a prayer half-said, and a heart half-gone.

And then there were mornings the coffee tasted like truce. Hands reached. Apologies learned the long road to the mouth. Therapy wasn't a magic wand. It was a shovel. We dug. slowly. We unlearned the language of defensiveness and learned the dialect of repair. We chose to stay when it would have been easier to run, and sometimes we chose to walk away from the same fights we used to sprint toward. Love is a stubborn work. On some days, survival is the romance.

If your marriage is a battlefield with a garden somewhere under the smoke, water the garden even if the sky is black. Ask for help. Set boundaries so fierce even your fear respects them. And if leaving is the safest and holiest thing you can do, leave with your head up. Boldness isn't always staying. Sometimes boldness is choosing peace in a different house.

Panic's Hands

No one sees panic until it's wearing your face. For me, it was the grocery store aisle that started shrinking, the car that turned coffin on the freeway, and the midnight heart pounding like it wanted out. I've been the woman in the restroom stall, counting breaths while strangers wash their hands and try not to hear me fall apart.

If that is you, the one who tastes metal when nothing's in your mouth, who checks the door lock three times because your chest says danger, I see you. Here is my unglamorous truth: Grounding saved me more times than prayers I couldn't remember in the moment. Five things I can see. Four things I can feel. Three things I can hear. Two things I can smell. One thing I can taste. Then the prayer. Always the prayer: "God, be near." He always was. Even when panic said He wasn't.

The Chemistry of Chemo and Choosing a Mirror

Chemo rooms smell like antiseptics and stubbornness. There's the sharp scent of cleaner, yes, but also the quieter smell of resolve. The way courage probably smells if it had a smell. The nurse would hang the bag. The drip would begin. My mouth would taste like pennies. Time would slow into a strange kindness, like it was tired, too.

I made a decision early: I would look in mirrors. Not to punish myself, but to witness myself. Some women choose scarves, some buzz their heads, some refuse to look, and some stare until they are familiar again. Every choice is holy. Mine was to make soup, paint my lips, cry, put on earrings, and go to war dressed like a woman who has already won.

I learned which days I could walk the block, and which days the block would walk me. I learned the sacredness of naps. I learned that hair grows back or it doesn't, and either way, I am not my follicles. I am not the dosage. I am not the chart. I am my children's mother. I am my husband's storm and shelter. I am God's stubborn daughter with a soft mouth and a steel spine.

The Stalkers and the Soft Target

No one wants to write about being hunted. But I promised you raw, so here it is: Visibility can paint a target. The more stages I stood on, the more cameras I faced, the more strangers felt licensed to trespass. Some slid into DMs. Some found emails. One or two found sidewalks. The body remembers all of it.

I tightened security. I changed routines. I learned to scan rooms without looking like I was scanning rooms. I told the truth to the authorities and to myself. And I refused to let fear evict my calling. If you are a woman whose success drew shadows to your door, know this: Your brilliance is not an invitation to harm. Get help. Document everything. And remember that choosing safety is not the same as choosing silence.

The Day the Pen Became a Sword

Grief still lived under my skin when I found a pen that didn't run out of ink. That day wasn't dramatic. No angels sang. I sat at a table, the kind with crumbs from last night and a vase that needed water, and I wrote one sentence like a dare. Then another. The words didn't fix me. They found me.

I wrote until my hand cramped. I wrote until my sadness had somewhere to go that wasn't my ribcage. And then I decided to build a bridge for other women to cross. One anthology turned into dozens. Then into a publishing house. Then into thirteen magazines with glossy pages that carried names no one had bothered to print before. Then into a TV network, red carpets, reporters with microphones, lights and gowns, and the holy hush after a good question.

People ask how. As if there's a hack. I tell them the truth they don't want because it isn't sexy: I kept going when I was tired. I asked for help when I didn't want to. I learned while doing. I apologized when I missed it. I delivered when it mattered most. I built a table, then added leaves, then pushed the walls back. I made room.

Plan A, Tattooed on the Heart

Plan A isn't a slogan. It's a scar you kiss every morning. It's a vow you renew when the sun is ugly and the mirror is mean. It's the decision to bet on what God put in your hands, not on what people put in your way.

I didn't make a Plan B because Plan B would have eaten Plan A in its sleep. If you leave the back door open, the wolves use it. Close the door. Nail it shut. When doubt knocks, send faith to answer. When failure texts, don't reply. When fear schedules a meeting, decline with delight.

Am I telling you to ignore risk? No. I am telling you to respect it and leap anyway. Risk is the toll on the bridge between where you are and who you said you would be.

If You've Been Where I've Been

If you have a father-shaped hole, if hands trespassed on sacred ground, if a nursery sits quiet, if your marriage breathes on a ventilator, if cancer signed your name without your consent, if panic crawls under your skin, if fame flirted and danger turned up, I won't give you Instagram wisdom here.

I will give you the only map that has worked for me. Not a tidy framework. A lived one:

- Tell the truth out loud. To someone safe. Shame dies when it's named.

- Choose a ritual that keeps you human. Prayer. Journaling. Walking. Stirring big pots of soup. Folding warm laundry. Call it boring. I call it survival.
- Make one brave phone call. The therapist. The lawyer. The doctor. The friend who answers at 2 am.
- Build a small altar to the life you are choosing. A candle. A verse. A picture. Light it when the house is dark.
- Say no without a thesis. "No" is complete. So is "I changed my mind."
- Ask for money without apologizing. Your gifts are not a favor. They're a service. Charge accordingly.
- Practice one tiny visibility habit. One 60-second video a week. One post that doesn't use a filter. One pitch to a podcast. One email to a magazine (mine or someone else's). Repeat.
- Write even when you hate your own voice. The page doesn't need you pretty. It needs you to be present.

This is not everything. It is enough to start. Start is where most women die. Don't.

Faith, Not as Performance but Pulse

I don't wear my faith like a billboard. I wear it like a pulse. It is there even when I don't point at it. Some days it is a shout, some days a rasp. Often, it's just breath. I have prayed furious prayers. I have prayed boring prayers. I have prayed, "If You're there, please be here." He was.

Scripture found me in hospital chairs and courthouse elevators. Not as a weapon against other people, but as a shield over my mind. "I will not die but live and declare the works of the Lord," I spoke that when the statistics said otherwise. "When I am afraid, I put my trust in You," I said that when fear took my keys. "He restores my soul." I clung to that when sleep wouldn't come.

If faith has felt like a country you got deported from, let me be your smuggler. We will cross back with nothing but honesty and a scrap of hope. God has never needed us to be polished to love us. Bare is good. Bare is a beginning.

The Work of Becoming Known

People imagine that "being known" is about followers. Followers are a metric. Being known is about impact. Who would miss you if you went quiet? That's your influence. Build that.

How did I build mine?

One woman at a time. One story at a time. One pitch at a time. One event at a time. I said yes to small rooms and did not despise them. I treated the handful like a multitude until it became one. I did not wait to be discovered. I documented my becoming. I did not wait for permission. I wrote my own.

The mechanics matter: the PR, the media kit, the one-sheet, the outreach cadence, the brand voice, and the AI tools that help when your brain is smoked. But the heart matters more. People don't remember perfectly. They remember the truth. They remember the woman who bled on a page and built a bridge with her bandages.

A 7-Day Reckless Hope Challenge (Do It With Me)

This is not a cute challenge. It's survival with a schedule. Start whenever you read this. If you miss a day, do the next one. No guilt, just grit.

Day 1 — Tell: Record a 60-second video telling one truth you've never said publicly. Post it or keep it. But say it out loud.

Day 2 — Write: Free-write for 10 minutes about the thing you lost. Don't edit. Print it. Hold it. You lived it.

Day 3 — Ask: Send one pitch (podcast, magazine, local TV, community stage). One.

Day 4 — Move: Walk for 20 minutes. Cry if you must. Pray if you can. Put your face in the sun.

Day 5 — Build: Create a simple one-sheet: photo, 50-word bio, 3 topics, contact. Imperfection is perfect.

Day 6 — Cut: Say no to one thing that drains you. Don't justify it.

Day 7 — Name: Write the sentence you want on your legacy: "I will be known for _____." Put it on your mirror.

Do this challenge every month until your life looks like a loud yes.

A Prayer for the Woman Who Thinks She Can't

God, for the one who can't find her breath, lend her Yours. For the one whose childhood still knocks at midnight, answer the door with mercy. For the one whose baby is in heaven, tuck her in on the nights when photos cut like glass. For the one in the infusion chair, make the drip holy. For the one whose marriage is a house of echoes, teach the walls to listen. For the one who thinks her voice is too small, turn it into a bell that calls her home. Amen.

The Vows I Keep (and You Can, Too)

I vowed to tell the truth, even when it costs me a room.

I vowed to choose Plan A, even when Plan B brings cupcakes.

I vowed to treat my body like a country I refuse to abandon.

I vowed to charge fairly and give generously.

I vowed to be a safe place for women's stories.

I vowed to stay when it's holy and go when it's necessary.

I vowed to live out loud because whispers never moved mountains.

Write your vows. Keep them in your wallet. Break them and rebuild them if you must. But have them. They will hold you when your hands can't.

What I Know Now

I know that absence can raise you as well as presence.

I know that what tried to end you becomes your dialect of compassion.

I know that money obeys assignments, not anxiety.

I know that visibility is not vanity: It is the stewardship of gifts, of message, of mission.

I know that God wastes nothing. Not even the darkest rooms. Especially not the darkest rooms.

To the Girl I Was (and the Woman You Are)

To the girl counting tiles on the ceiling: Your body is not a crime scene. It is a cathedral. The door will open. You will walk out.

To the young mother with the empty blanket: You are still a mother. Love didn't die in that room. It relocated.

To the wife with a suitcase in the trunk and a prayer on her tongue: You will know what to do. Your peace will tell you. Listen.

To the patient in the chair: The needle is not the narrator. You are.

To the woman who wants to burn it all down: Maybe you need a match. Maybe you need a map. Either way, you will not stay lost.

To you, reading this and wondering if I am talking to someone else. I am not. I am talking to you. Because you are the reason I write, the reason I build tables, the reason I turn my own pain into lumber and lay it down as a bridge.

The Last Door

If I could take you to one moment that changed everything, it would not be the red carpet or the book hitting a list. It would be the afternoon I closed the last door to Plan B. I turned the deadbolt. I slid the chain. I taped a note: "Do not reopen." I sat on the floor on the other side and shook, because certainty is a myth and faith is a muscle that trembles when you finally use it.

Then I stood up. I opened my laptop. I wrote to a woman I hadn't met yet and told her that her story mattered. She wrote back. The next day, five more did. Then fifty. Then five hundred. And suddenly I was not alone, and neither were they.

That is the miracle we get to participate in: We don't climb out of the pit just to admire the sky. We throw down ropes. We become ladders. We teach other women how to tie knots with their own hands.

Live It Out Loud: A Declaration

I will plan a life I love and live it out loud.

I will be the loudest kind of gentle and the gentlest kind of loud.

I will not apologize for surviving.

I will not whisper when hell needs to hear me.

I will make art with my scars.

I will be known, not for being untouchable, but for being unafraid to be touched by life and still rise.

I will be a mother to my children and a midwife to women's dreams.

I will build tables and pull up chairs and teach women to carve their names into the wood.

I will keep my vows. I will keep my faith. I will keep going.

If you want to know how I did it, here it is: I kept going. I kept going when I had every reason to stop. I kept going when my hands shook and my eyes burned and my bank account sneered and my past jeered and my body begged for a softer story. I kept going because a softer story would have been a smaller life. And I promised that girl in the hallway with the door clicking shut that I would build her a bigger one.

So I did. So I am. So will you.

Plan A. Out loud. Boldly.

Always.

Hanna

Gabby Gutierrez

The beauty of success by Gabby G
Inspirational, motivational life and business coach and
a Brand Ambassador

http://www.linkedin.com/in/gabby-gutierrez-b16ab736
https://www.facebook.com/gabby.gutierrez.9081
https://www.instagram.com/gabbygu9/
https://thebeautyofsuccess.com/

Gabby Gutierrez is a passionate and determined woman who has devoted her life to helping others discover their purpose, embrace their potential, and create lives filled with joy and fulfillment. With over 30 years of experience as a successful entrepreneur, Gabby has influenced and inspired thousands of women worldwide, guiding them to rise above challenges and step boldly into their own power.

As one of the top leaders in the company she represents, Gabby has proven that resilience, dedication, and heart-driven leadership can transform not only businesses but also lives. Her journey has been shaped by personal experiences that she now channels into empowering others—turning every lesson into an opportunity to serve, uplift, and guide.

Fueled by an unwavering passion for personal development, Gabby is constantly exploring new ways to support and inspire those around her. Whether through her writing, mentorship, or leadership, her mission remains clear: to help people unlock their fullest potential and live happier, more purposeful lives.

From Shattered Dreams to the Courage to Begin Again: A Journey of Resilience

By Gabby Gutierrez

The Shattering Moment

There are times in life when everything changes in an instant. One moment you're standing, the next it feels like the ground has been pulled out from under you. For me, that moment was finding out that my husband of twenty years had been unfaithful (something that maybe I didn't want to realize even though there were signs long before). After two decades of building a life together, raising dreams, and imagining our future, the truth hit me like a storm I never saw coming.

It felt like my whole world stopped. My heart sank so deep I wondered if I would ever feel whole again. Suddenly, everything I thought I knew about my future was gone. The life I had pictured — growing old together, sharing milestones — disappeared in a single moment.

The pain of betrayal is hard to put into words. It's not just about losing a marriage; it's about losing the "us" that defined so much of your identity. Who was I without that story? What did my future look like now?

The nights were the hardest. Alone with my thoughts, I asked every *"what if"* and *"why me"* question possible. I cried until there were no tears left, and then I just lay there in silence, staring at the ceiling, feeling like I had nothing left to give.

What I didn't expect was how betrayal affects every part of you — body, mind, and spirit. My chest felt heavy all the time, like I couldn't breathe deeply. My thoughts spun in circles I couldn't stop. Even food lost its taste, joy lost its color, and the simplest tasks felt impossible. Heartbreak doesn't just stay in the heart — it shows up in every part of your life.

Living in the Aftermath

The days after the truth came out were some of the hardest of my life. It's not like you wake up the next morning ready to start over. Instead, you wake up and remember — again — that everything has changed.

Life didn't pause for me to catch my breath. Bills still had to be paid. My business still needed me. My family still leaned on me. And on top of it all, I had to move to a new city to be closer to a sick parent and my family. Hiding everything I was going through made things even harder. My plate wasn't just full — it was overflowing.

Most days I felt like I was running on fumes. On the outside, I smiled, ran meetings, and showed up for others. On the inside, I was shattered. It felt like trying to run a marathon with a broken leg — painful and exhausting.

But in that season, I learned something: Resilience doesn't always look strong. Sometimes it looks like showing up while your heart is in pieces. Sometimes, it looks like whispering a prayer through tears, or dragging yourself out of bed when you want to hide.

The hardest part wasn't just the work or the responsibilities — it was the mask. Pretending everything was fine while I was breaking inside. Smiling for others, then crying in the car. Leading my business while wondering if I could even lead myself. Carrying other people's burdens while mine felt too heavy to lift. Hiding pain may feel easier in the moment, but it's exhausting for the soul. It was in those hidden moments that I began to realize how desperately I needed God to carry what I couldn't.

I had no strength left, but somehow God's grace kept me going. Not a month at a time, not even a week at a time — just enough for the day.

Wrestling with God

When life knocks the wind out of you, it's normal to ask God hard questions. I sure did.

Why me? Why now? Haven't I trusted You enough?

Most of the time, I didn't get an answer. The silence felt unbearable. But looking back, I see that God was speaking — just not in the ways I expected. Sometimes, it was through a song that played at just the right moment. Sometimes, it was through a verse that jumped off the page. Sometimes, it was through a friend calling out of nowhere to pray with me. Messages and signs were everywhere, all the time.

And here's what I learned in the silence: God isn't always in the lightning or thunder. Sometimes He's in the whisper. He doesn't always give us explanations, but He always offers His presence. And in the long nights when I thought He was absent, I now see He was the one holding me together. The silence wasn't abandonment — it was an invitation to trust deeper.

I realized God isn't afraid of our doubts, our tears, or even our anger. He wants us to leave everything up to Him. And slowly, my question changed from *"Why did this happen?"* to *"God, what can You do with this?"*

One Day at a Time

The idea of rebuilding my whole life was overwhelming. So God reminded me: *You don't have to do it all at once — just take the next step.*

Some days, the next step was as simple as making coffee or answering one email. Other days, it was showing up to lead when my heart wasn't in it. Courage didn't look glamorous back then. It looked messy. It looked like whispered prayers and shaky hands. But it was still courage.

Matthew 6:34 became my survival plan: *"Do not worry about*

tomorrow... each day has enough trouble of its own." I stopped trying to figure out how I'd survive the year and focused on surviving the day.

And little by little, the days got lighter.

Rebuilding Myself

When the marriage ended, I had to face a scary question: *Who am I now?* For years, my identity was tied to "us." Without that, I felt lost. But slowly, I realized this wasn't just an ending — it was an invitation to rediscover myself. I learned to enjoy my own company, made new routines, and started dreaming again. I poured into my business, not to escape, but to remind myself I still had purpose.

Isaiah 61:3 promises "beauty for ashes." My life felt like ashes, but God was making something beautiful out of it.

I discovered my worth was never in a marriage. It was in the One who created me.

The Power of Faith and Resilience

The truth is, resilience isn't about never falling apart. It's about rising again with God's help.

What amazed me most was how, even while I was broken, God used me to encourage others. Sometimes I'd be speaking hope into someone else's life, and it hit me — *the very hope I'm giving them is the hope I still need myself.*

Romans 8:28 says, *"In all things God works for the good of those who love him."* At first, I couldn't imagine how my pain could be used for good. But over time, I saw how my story encouraged others to keep going through their storms.

Faith gave my resilience roots. Without God, I might have pushed through with willpower, but I would have burned out. With Him, I didn't just survive — I was transformed.

A New Beginning

Eventually, I realized: I made it. I survived what I thought would break me.

This wasn't the life I planned, but it was still a good life. In fact, it was a chance to live more authentically, more courageously, and more in tune with God's purpose for me.

Jeremiah 29:11 became a promise I held close: *"For I know the plans I have for you... plans to give you hope and a future."*

And He did just that. He gave me new dreams, new courage, and new joy. My past didn't define me — His love did.

A Word for You

If you are reading this and find yourself in the middle of your own storm, I want you to know something: You are not alone. I know what it feels like to have your world shatter, to carry a heart that feels too heavy to hold, and to wonder if you'll ever feel whole again.

I know what it feels like to have your heart shattered. But I also know this: You will get through it. Not because you're super strong, but because God is. He hasn't left you, even if you can't feel Him right now.

Take it one day at a time. Don't try to rebuild your whole future today — just take the next small step. Cry if you need to. Rest when you must. But never lose sight of this truth: Your story isn't over.

God will take your ashes and turn them into something beautiful. He will turn your pain into purpose. He will use even this season — the one you wish you could skip — to grow you into someone stronger, wiser, and more resilient than you ever imagined.

Here are a few simple things that helped me:

1. *Writing down one thing I was grateful for each night, even if it was small. Reading a verse aloud every morning, even when I didn't feel like it. Reaching out to one trusted friend instead of isolating. These little steps didn't erase the pain, but they gave me strength to keep going. Try one small step today — and let God meet you there.*

2. My prayer for you is Romans 15:13: *"May the God of hope fill you with all joy and peace as you trust in him, so that you may overflow with hope."*

3. Hold on to hope. Believe in His promises. And remember, even in the darkest chapters, God is writing a story of redemption and new beginnings for you.

Carmen Maendel

Co-CEO of Nate's Property Maintenance LLC

https://www.linkedin.com/in/carmen-maendel-17510944/
https://www.facebook.com/ncmaendel
https://www.instagram.com/maendelcarmen/
https://natespropertymaintenance.com
https://courageouswoman.net

Hello I'm Carmen Maendel. Nate and I are a husband and wife team. Our fifteen year old son, Josh officially works for our company as well. We have embarked upon an entrepreneurial journey together that is extremely rewarding for all of us. We own and operate Nate's Property Maintenance LLC together. I handle the business on the home front while my husband coordinates our projects on the job sites with our clients and team of workers. We compliment each other very well working together, and remain very service oriented in our company. Some of the business roles I perform are the following: balancing our books, regularly posting to social media, scheduling our clients, arranging purchase contracts for new business equipment, keeping our business licenses and registration up to date, documenting client files, and much more. Nate works with our clients by coordinating all the projects and equipment on the job sites and carefully plans for each of our projects we do down to the finest of details.

Windows into My Soul

By Carmen Maendel

ENIGMA

Splishing, splashing, ripping, thrashing
wind envelopes the ocean floor.
Tugging, pulling, rising, falling
bottle floats upon the shore;
within that bottle has in store...
That paper so sacred

What does it reveal
To whom shall it appeal
That paper so sacred

Wishing, hoping, missing, groping
bottle burrows in the sand.
In, out, backwards, forward
moves the bottle by command;
swiftly through this promised land...
That paper so sacred

Laughing, crying, living, dying
paper hides within its walls
Secure, afraid, vibrant, dull
implied feeling is that all;
bottle lets out a call...

That paper so sacred

What does it reveal
To whom shall it appeal
That paper so sacred

Winning, losing, relaxing, grueling
determined by life, the game
Boast, squeal, play, work
the questions answered never same;
secret kept in bottle frame...
That paper so sacred

What does it reveal
To whom shall it appeal
That paper so sacred

Sneaking, lurking, prowling creeping
impends upon the assailable glass
hover, retreat, naïve, all-knowing
thief approaches near to pass;
hurdles bottle with a crash...
That paper so sacred

What does it reveal
To whom shall it appeal
That paper so sacred

Misjudging, puzzling, avoiding, deceiving
foolish eyes are opened wide
confront, escape, resist, concur
rules of life must abide;
now exposed can not hide...
This paper so sacred

What does it reveal
To whom shall it appeal
This paper so sacred

Plunging, succeeding, exploding, believing
paper emerges from the shore
acquire, achieve, ascend, defeat
thief captures life no more...
This paper so sacred

- Carmen K. Phelps (Maendel), 1995
Timeless Voices Copyright 2006 The International Library of Poetry as
a compilation

Bottle - Paper - Door

Why do I begin here?

Enigma - a one-page poem revealing the mysterious conundrum of
the transition between childhood and adulthood - depicts the deep
mysteries and anticipations about the innocence of growing up. I
wrote this poem while I was still in college, and envisioned myself
progressing through the various stages of life; including all unknowns,
predictabilities, and self-discoveries. Mainly, *"the paper so sacred"* is

the key to many *doors* we walk through in life. As we close one door, God opens another for us, as it is said *"I know your deeds. See, I have placed before you an open door that no one can shut. I know that you have little strength, yet you have kept my word (Revelation 3:8)."* Each *bottle* belongs to a unique individual, and it is up to that person to interpret the encrypted message on the paper within the bottle frame.

As I reflect back to this time of life, I was in the middle of my long term "career" as a student. I had graduated from Cornell College and was attending the undergraduate program at UW Madison for Speech and Language Pathology. I had so many dreams and aspirations at this point in time, and was anxious to finish my program and discover everything "the world" had for me. I also did not know Jesus or have the same personal relationship I do with Him today. I was too engrossed with getting degrees and making money at that point of my life.

The Long Downhill and The Hand of God

Several things happened while I was in college that derailed me from the course I was heading. My best friend, Christine, was in a serious car accident together with her little brother, Shore, and his fiancé, Kara; who were both killed in this accident. My best friend ended up in a coma for that entire summer of 1992. I remember visiting her daily with her mom at the hospital, and hoping that she would come back to all of us. Her mom stayed with my mother and I in Iowa City that summer so that she could be close to her daughter in the hospital. She did come out of her coma and we have remained very close friends up to this day. The little brother "Shore" of my best friend was my "first love."

Over time, our relationship transitioned into more of a brotherly-sisterly one because I spent so much time with their family growing up. I always knew that I would be happy for him wherever he ended up in life. However, I neither expected, nor even prepared for him to die so early in life. This year was very traumatic for me, and it would take longer years ahead to heal from this pain. Holding on to this Scripture has provided me comfort and strength: "*Trust in the LORD with all your heart and lean not on your own understanding; in all your ways submit to him, and he will make your paths straight (Proverbs 3: 5-6)*".

Around that same time, my father was battling with his "fifteen or so years" of cancer. There were so many unknowns in my life, and now that young woman, in me, that was ready to take on the world did not even know where she belonged or fit into this world. I started on a downward spiral and began to use the vending machines at college for meals, and late night pizza runs became the norm. I switched my major from pre-med to art and business at that time. I struggled with every single relationship in my life including friends, parents, my boyfriend, my parents and grandparents. I knew there had to be more in life than feeling the way I did then, and I made it my life's mission to discover "something more" in life.

I finished my "career" as a student and was ready to face reality. I taught Special Education courses in the south for several years while married to my first husband. We mutually parted ways after seven years of marriage, and I was starting fresh out west now. It was here in Colorado Springs that things began to change in my life. I left my teaching position due to not being able to get my teaching contract renewed. Everyone else was older than me and had tenure, however that was not the case for me. It just happened that one of the mothers of the students I taught in high school for math and English was the Executive Director of Edward Jones. I was interviewed by their investment firm several times with a panel, and was finally offered the position of financial advisor and stock broker with their firm shortly after that. I successfully passed the Series 7 and 63 exams, and my eight-year-long career in financial services began. I used to have dollar signs in my eyes, and was prepared to make my millions which also made my family extremely proud. That's when I realized that God had a different plan for my life.

I first met my husband and love of my life, Nathanael (Nate) Maendel around that same time. He would come into the bank where I was working and visit regularly. My co-workers would always tell me, *"What about him? He seems to be taking an interest in you?"* I simply viewed Nate as a very close friend of mine then. We initially met at Woodmen Valley Church in their singles group, *Mosaic.* We still laugh about the fact that I turned him down three times when he had asked for my phone number. What I did not know at the time was that he was in charge of connecting people that visited our singles group through attaining their phone, email, and contact information. Nate viewed me as a "high-falutin" stock broker at that time and nothing else. It was not until later that year that Mosaic started meeting on Sunday mornings after church, instead of evenings, which made Nate and I reacquainted again.

I remember the first time I returned to *Mosaic* on a Sunday and walked right up to him. He was making the necessary preparations to the sound system before church started that day. There was a faint hint of praise and worship music playing in the background. I proceeded to ask him, *"Do you remember me?"* I got a half-interested and slightly annoyed response from him, *"Yes, I do."* I remember glancing over at him while he was running the soundboard equipment and thinking, *"We are going to get married someday."* Somehow we moved past that first awkward hello and started to meet after church for Starbucks coffee. These Starbucks outings grew longer as we were starting to get to know each other on a deeper level. The Scripture from 1 John 4:16 mentioning that *"God is love"* being the central aspect of my relationship with Him and others is also the same love that drew Nate and I closer to one another.

What I did not realize is that God had a plan to use Nate and two other women as a conduit to help bring me back to Him. I came to the Lord when I was a teenager, but my indifference had blinded me to acknowledge God's divine intervention. I still remember Nate standing at the entrance of the clubs I was dancing at, without entering himself, as if to draw me away from that atmosphere. He would also change the music settings in my JAG to Christian music. We started to attend weekly Bible studies together and went out in groups to Christian comedy shows. We began spending more time together and talking about tentative future plans together. I rededicated my life to Jesus Christ on November 4, 2006. I shared my unforgettable experience that night in my Chapter: "The Evening that Completely Transformed My Life - November 4, 2006" in the Anthology: A Season to Remember - Holiday, just in case you would like to read more about this incredible evening that changed my life forever.

We started officially courting one another and made various trips to Minnesota and Iowa to visit our families. When Nate and I were visiting Iowa one time, Nate planted yellow daffodils in the shape of a heart and requested my hand in marriage from my dad and step-mom. Every Spring, those beautiful fragrant yellow daffodils pop out of the ground to say, "Hello." My step-mother shares a photo with me annually to commemorate that beautiful moment where she, Nate, and my dad planted those together in their back field.

I believe that God was guiding and directing Nate and I to the life we have today. As said from Romans 8:28, "*And we know that for those who love God all things work together for good, for those who are called according to his purpose.*" We were married in Waterloo, Iowa on July 21, 2007, and our son, Josh was born a few years later on January 23, 2009. God was guiding and directing us along the way. Our favorite verses were Proverbs 3:5-6 and Isaiah 40:31 (*But those who wait for the LORD shall renew their strength; they shall mount up with wings like eagles; they shall run and not be weary; they shall walk and not faint*) which became our guide in the next few years in our lives.

God has helped us through numerous occasions that we always refer back to these verses to find comfort and refuge in Him, particularly the time when we lost our twins and another baby shortly after, during mid-pregnancy. The memory still lingers in me like it happened only yesterday. Nate and I will probably never fully recover from this loss. God still continues to encourage and heal our hearts during times of broken dreams and parenthood. We also traveled down the road to adoption several times, however, the situation and timing never seemed to be a good fit. Still, we put our trust in God's hands because He is in complete and utter control over this and everything else in our lives. As Proverbs 16:9 says, *"In their hearts, humans plan their course, but the Lord establishes their steps."*

My view of entrepreneurship has shifted dramatically since my "stock broker" days, and I now view business, money, our possessions, relationships, and everything else very differently than I once did. I now own/co-own four businesses in the last twelve years and currently operate Nate's Property Maintenance LLC with my husband. God is the true owner of everything in our lives.

We simply need to be good stewards of all the blessings and resources that God blesses us with. He knows everything in advance so there is no need to attempt to hide anything from Him. This should provide a sense of security, reassurance, and comfort that surpasses all understanding.

God is my everything today. He is my comforter, healer, reassurance, peace, protector, and my all in all. I will continue to place my full trust in Jesus Christ regardless of my circumstances. Thus, *"And we know that for those who love God all things work together for good, for those who are called according to his purpose (Romans 8:18)."*

LOOK AWAY

When I look at you
I am reminded of Him
Looking deep in your eyes

It's no great surprise
Like quicksand, you are luring me in

Looking away due to the pain
How can I ever explain?

When we lock eyes
It's no great surprise
I am falling in
Rescue me now please

Help me look away
Help me not stay
Help me turn to you God
Help me pray

When I look at you
I am reminded of Him
Looking deep in your eyes
It's no great surprise
Like a magnetic force, you are luring me in

Looking away due to the pain
How can I ever explain?

Knowing that was then
This is now
Never can be again
Time can't rewind

When I look at you
I am reminded of Him
Looking deep in your eyes

It's no great surprise
Like a tidal wave, you are luring me in

Looking away due to the pain
How can I ever explain?

Please let me go
You left long ago
Stop haunting me with those eyes
Tears are long gone and completely dried

When I look at you
I am reminded of Him
Looking deep in your eyes
It's no great surprise
Like a smorgasbord of treats, you are luring me in

Looking away due to the pain
How can I ever explain?

Traveling deep to your soul
Fully transparent
Completely exposed
Remembering how sweet it was long ago

When I look at you
I am reminded of Him
Looking deep in your eyes
It's no great surprise
Like a sweet song, you are luring me in

Looking away due to the pain
How can I ever explain?

My passionate imploding heart
Can't take anymore
Please release me from your grip
Allow me to truly live

When I look at you
I am reminded of Him
Looking deep in your eyes
It's no great surprise
Like a fatal attraction, you are luring me in

Looking away due to the pain
How can I ever explain?

"Thank you Lord for helping me keep my eyes on You!"

- Carmen K. Maendel Copyright 2019

Look Away / Look Toward God

The world has a strange way of trying to pull you back into it, and I find myself always in need to be in the Word, surrounded by like-minded Christians, our church family, and other Christian influences to remain firmly planted and grounded in Jesus Christ. Psalms 16:8 (*I keep my eyes always on the LORD. With him in my right hand, I will not be shaken*) became my shelter. I find it funny how you can be going along in life normally, and then you meet someone that suddenly triggers old feelings of something that maybe never was said out loud. It happened to me when I met someone that reminded me of someone from my past. I knew, logically, that this person was not the same person that I knew. They looked the same, acted the same, and even had a similar personality. So, I "looked away" to protect my heart and soul.

Living in the past is no good for anyone. It draws your focus and attention away from the present, and robs you and others from the "new" moments and memories with the people close to you. Based on the movie, Kung Fu Panda, out of Oogway's mouth, "Yesterday is history, tomorrow is a mystery, but today is a gift. That is why we call it the present." Every day is a gift and we should be investing it in the Kingdom of Heaven instead of in this world, as everything else will eventually turn to dust, and the investments we do for the Kingdom of Heaven will last for an eternity.

The last poem that I will share in this chapter is "Look Away." It has a dual meaning. The "Him" in the poem is the world and all the worldly influences that can sweep a person away from Christ like materialism, greed, lust, etc. In the same token, it also means to stand strong in Christ and not let these influences rob your mind, heart, body, spirit, and soul. It serves as a reminder of where I came from and where I never want to return to. I want to emulate Christ and become more like Him each day.

We are blessed so that we can bless others. We, as a couple, look for those amazing opportunities to reach out and help others whether it is our clients, friends, family, church family, business colleagues, and complete strangers. Nate and I would love to start a *pay it forward movement* that simply means helping others through discovering your own spiritual gifts and sharing them with everyone you meet.

As I reflect on our company and what we have built and scaled tremendously over the last two or so years after becoming an LLC, I realized how God has had His hand over us to bless our company. So, Nate and I are always looking for ways to give back and pay it forward in life. We regularly go out to restaurants and pick out a single mom with kids, a couple, or sometimes an entire family to bless with a meal. Not too long ago we did this for a family at Apple Bee's. The family was so touched that they wanted to take a picture of themselves and our group as a keepsake. We usually do this anonymously and it was so fulfilling to watch their grateful expressions when they received a free meal from us. We continually look for opportunities to do this whether it be paying for someone's groceries anonymously, or just even by simply addressing our waiter/waitress by their name.

Paying it forward is not always done by monetary means. Another way to pay it forward without spending money is doing volunteer work through helping someone do something or visiting someone. Our time and service are also gifts to others. More so, we regularly look for opportunities to refer businesses out to other companies in various areas we do business with. When we receive a lead that is outside of our normal scope of work, we will be pleased to pass it along to help others build their companies as well, because we see other tree companies in the area as our colleagues and friends, too, instead of our competition. Kindness is free and it always comes back to us tenfold. Nate and I will continue to be the hands and feet of Jesus to others.

"The King will reply, 'Truly I tell you, whatever you did for one of the least of these brothers and sisters of mine, you did for me (Matthew 25:40)."

"LOOK AWAY"

Always best to focus on the here and the now and your future. Leave the past in the past!

I encourage you to discover your own *paper* held within the bottle frame!

Carmen Maendel

COURAGEOUS WOMAN CASTING
CARES UPON JESUS

Powered by MySignature.io

Kali Morris

Founder of Wealth IV Generations

Kali Morris is a seasoned, state licensed, federally compliant financial professional, with years of experience in the financial services industry. Specializing in wealth accumulation, asset protection, and increasing net worth. Kali has a long track record of guiding clients to achieve their financial goals. Throughout her career she has demonstrated exceptional analytical skills and understanding of her clients' needs and wants. She believes that no one should work 40 to 50 years and not enjoy their hard-earned money. She made it her mission to get you to your perfect retirement destination by design.

https://www.linkedin.com/in/kholoud-morris-37bb05132/
https://www.facebook.com/kali.morris.2025/
https://www.instagram.com/kali.morris_wealth4generations/
https://kalimorris.mynewretirement.com/
https://kalimorris.com/

Dare to Dream Again!

By Kali Morris

"You can't do that!" Those words slapped me so many times.

"You can't color your hair!" *"You can't pursue your education unless we approve!"* *"You can't date! It's forbidden!"*

I remember the voices. There are so many *"can't do that!"* ... I was barely alive. My life, my hopes, my dreams were being drained out of me. A whole society was purposefully diminishing me as a woman.

I was born and raised in Saudi Arabia in a time when women did not drive or work without permission. Marriages were mostly arranged at a young age (as early as 9-12 years old), and schools were segregated by gender (and still are in 2025). The number of women-only gyms or swimming pools in the country could be counted on one hand; modesty was enforced only for women in that male-dominated society. It was truly a man's world.

I wished upon all wishes to be free of all the *"cant's."* Secretly, I kindled a flame: I had to escape! I was desperate for a way out.

I found refuge in books on success. Stealing away to read them when not studying my textbooks. Countless times, I woke up with a personal development book under my cheek, having fallen asleep in the midst of reading. Dreaming. Planning. Taking quiet steps...

Personal development drove me. It was hope spurred on by consistent action. Small, but steady steps forward.

At 27 years old, my time had come, and the door of opportunity had finally opened. It was another battle to find the courage to walk through it, but I said, *"Enough is enough!"* No more *"cant's."* I was granted a full scholarship to study in the US, and I was going to accept it and convince my father to give me his legal consent. I had been saving the money I would need and applying to colleges. Once I was accepted, I got my Visa, and with perseverance, I cleared all the other obstacles that were between me and my goal, except for male permission part. In the end, my father granted my wish, and I was free to start my new adventure.

I left my country of birth to come here, to America, to get my master's degree, and to make my own life happen. A life where permission came only from me.

My personal development journey continued. I read books, attended seminars, took online courses, and participated in mastermind events. I felt I had the recipe for success! I broke out, made decisions, and fell flat on my face. I got chewed up and spit out by the new world. Made some good choices and made some hellish mistakes. I suffered unpredictable outcomes. Yet, as I look back, I also was touched by unexpected joys.

Darkness did regain the light in my life sometimes, and so often I asked, *"Why is this happening to me?"* So much seemed to be beyond my control. There were so many scary moments, where more than once I believed it would truly kill me. But I never gave up. And because of this, my will to persevere grew stronger, and others saw that too.

Those times when I was at my wits' end, a moment would happen: a phone call, a suggestion, a friend from nowhere would help me. And again, a second time, I pulled myself from the darkness. From the pit I had fallen into. Because, though the spirit of one who strives might be put down, those strong of heart will always rise again.

Navigating my new life in the United States, I found out that we are not that different after all. Not that long ago, a new millennium – the year 2000 – celebrations lit up the skies all over the globe. Now, a quarter century later, some of us are still doing the same things.

How many years have you let slip away? Are you committed to your goals, or have you already given up on your dreams?

Have you gone back to your old ways? To the same old list of excuses: *I don't have time, I am busy* (with what? Or that sounds too hard compared to what?). Convincing yourself that you have no time today to add something new to your routine?

Some people are still doing the same things they've been complaining about for the past 25 years. Still saying they will take that trip, run that race, learn that instrument, or a second language. The list goes on and on. Will you wait until next year? Next year will never come. Some of us have forgotten about the lives we envisioned for ourselves. Do you know someone like that? Are you that person?

I believe we have all been there at some point in our lives, Others only dream about a life that they could live, but they do nothing about it! yet some of us have changed and decided to take charge of our lives, and refused to settle for what our life looks like today.

At the beginning of this year, there was a powerful day, January 20th, and no, not because it was a holiday for many of us. It serves as a special reminder of what it means to fight for your dreams. It is the day we celebrate the life of Dr. Martin Luther King, Jr. On August 28th, 1963, during his historic march on Washington, he called for civil and economic equal rights and an end to racism in the United States. The title of the speech that started it all was, "I Have a Dream." He dreamed that one day his children could live in a country where they would not be judged by the color of their skin, but by the content and the value that they provide to their community.

Today, we have a new type of segregation. Financial segregation. The top 10% vs. the other 90%. In the United States, you need a net worth of approximately $970,900[1] to enter the top 10%. You are not going to make it without a plan that you put into action.

Most people are not able to answer basic questions about their financial health.

What are your goals? What do you do for a living? How much income do you want? How healthy are your personal relationships? What are your relationship goals? How are your relationships with your kids? What hobbies are you enjoying? Who are your friends? What does your dream life look like? Where will you live? Are you thinking about all the memories you will create with your loved ones? Are you doing anything to move toward that beautiful future?

Have you illustrated a plan to reach your goals? Or is your life on repeat? Wake up, go to work, come home, eat dinner, watch TV, go to bed. Then repeat every day for the next 20 years. Until one day you lift your head up, look in the mirror, and you don't look at anything like you expected. You aren't living the life you dreamed for yourself. Why not? Maybe it is easier to simply lie to yourself: The dream life is not for you, it's for those who were born with a silver spoon in their mouths. You are a victim of your circumstances.

"By changing nothing, Nothing Changes!" - Tony Robbins.

Sadly, most people do not create a plan, make goals, or take action. They simply have wishes. They do not live their dream lives or have passionate, happy relationships. They are unhealthy and unfit, and have forgotten how to have fun. It's all survival mode. Most people do not have jobs they like, and they feel trapped. Do you know someone like that? Or might that be you?

Every day you wake up is a gift that has been given to you. Last night was the last night for some. One night will be the last night for you! Would you be happy with the life you lived? If yes, then you are doing great and do not need to change anything. But if you are not satisfied with where you are today, you have regrets, you want more, then you owe it to yourself to do something about it! You only get one life! What do you want to change?

Write down 5 to 10 goals. Are they realistic, measurable, and have you set a time to get them done? Can you assess the progress? If one of your goals is too big, split it into smaller, more manageable goals. That's what S.M.A.R.T goals look like: Specific, Measurable, Attainable, Relevant, Timely. Now ask yourself: Are they what you truly want? Are they worth the sacrifices you will need to make? Once you have answered these questions, there is no stopping you if you are consistent and determined to achieve your goals.

My professional advice for you is to write down your vision in detail. Write and write and write. When we write something down, research suggests that as far as our brain is concerned, it is as if we are actually doing it. If you are a "write-it-down" kind of person, you know how important this is, and you know how it works. If you are not, try it anyways and see the difference.

Read your written goals at least three times a day, and your brain will find the necessary steps to reach them. Use a planner or a journal to record how you spend your time. Track your income and expenses. See what has been stopping you from moving forward. Try this for the next 30 days. When you start to feel your life shifting *To A Better Future*, please share your success, and help someone else.

Do not be a statistic! In 2008, the Great Recession had a profound effect on the retirement savings and 401(k)s of many seniors.[2] In some cases, baby boomers nearing retirement saw losses of <u>over 40%</u>. Because of their age and proximity to retirement, they had a diminished ability to recover these losses. Although they had planned for a comfortable retirement, many baby boomers saw their hopes dashed in the aftermath of the 2008 financial crisis.

In 2022, retirees lost 23% of their 401(k) savings.[3] Please do not take my word for it, just take a look at who is handing out samples at Costco, or who is checking your receipt at Walmart. Watch as Winter approaches who is pushing a shopping cart when it is raining and windy. Is it an 18–21 year-old or is it a baby boomer, dealing with the pain of betrayal piercing through their everyday duties, just to put food on the table?

In 2017, I had my first child, and what a blessing he is. I wanted to give the world to him. I decided that we would live a comfortable life and never be in a position where I cannot provide that life for us. In California, that means I need to be financially independent, and I cannot simply rely on a steady paycheck. That is when my journey in the financial industry started.

I came from another continent, and spoke a different language. It is natural that I would need to learn the basics of finance. To my surprise, it was not just me, most of the population is in the dark. Coworkers, neighbors, and friends have told me the same thing. They do not know much about personal finance. A spouse or a paid accountant might handle it, so they think they do not need to understand. It made me curious why women who are born with many freedoms choose to ignore such an important one.

The Equal Credit Opportunity Act (ECOA),[4] enacted on October 28, 1974, is a federal law that prohibits discrimination in lending based on race, color, religion, national origin, sex, marital status, or age. Before this, women did not have the legal right to even own a bank account without the permission of a man. Think about it: The financial interests of women in the United States have only been protected by law for 50 years!

The statistics are even more shocking. Women are significantly less likely to negotiate salaries and ask for raises. These women are three times as likely as men to say they cannot afford to save for retirement, highlighting the need for better financial education. These statistics illustrate the ongoing challenges women face in the financial realm. My eyes searched for the *Oprah's* of the world. Between 2014 and 2019, there was a 21% increase in women-owned businesses, while all businesses increased by only 9%. Did they make a profit, did they still enjoy what they do?

At the other end of the spectrum, women in poverty are at a higher risk of experiencing domestic violence, and those who do may face severe economic consequences, including job loss and debt. Financial abuse is prevalent in domestic violence cases, often involving control over money, preventing employment, and creating dependency. Strengthening financial literacy support can help survivors break free from the cycle of abuse and rebuild their lives. Resources like the National Network to End Domestic Violence offer guidance and support for survivors facing financial challenges.

In 2018, I spent my first Mother's Day ever away from my son, to attend the first class I needed by the state of California to obtain my Financial Professional license. I vowed to be a beacon of light for all, to improve, if not dramatically transform, their financial situations. Fast-forward to 2025. My team and I are licensed in multiple states. We are certified to support our clients and their communities in financial matters ranging from pre- and post-retirement strategies, and tax-advantaged college savings plans which do not affect eligibility for financial aid or federal grants, as is the case with 529 plans and mutual funds. We specialize in wealth accumulation, asset protection, and strategies for business owners and many more.

I have hosted workshops and have been invited to speak at seminars. Sharing the story of my financial transformation and the positive impact which is building *Wealth IV Generations* to come.

Fasten your seat belts, this trip may get bumpy. Your thoughts will race at 200 mph. You will have so many questions! How long will it take? Is it worth starting now? Am I too late? Maybe I have more time? Do I need a living will? Aren't trusts only for wealthy people? They will keep flying in your mind, month after month, until you move past the fear of finding out where you are financially.

How much do I need for retirement? If something happens to me, will my family have a backup or guaranteed source of income? If I have a mortgage, would losing my job mean losing the house? What if I get injured?

Do you simply hope nothing happens, are you living paycheck to paycheck like 63% of Americans? Everyone wants a good life. All parents say they are willing to do what it takes for their kids. What about you? What are you willing to do for yourself? The answers to all of these questions can be determined by your habits and choices.

Self-discipline is self-love, and the road to sustained happiness is built with discipline. This is not about punishment, it is about forgoing immediate pleasure in exchange for long-term self-respect.

If a friend or a loved one asks for our help and support, we always manage to show a lot of care and a capacity to make changes that benefit them, and that is great because you are expressing how you feel about them. What about yourself?Do you show yourself that same level of love and kindness?

If we only express love on certain occasions, then we do not love ourselves enough. Show love every day, to others and yourself. I do not claim I am a love expert. I am a financial strategy expert. But I read the research that was conducted by experts, and they conclude that the most fulfillment results from loving humanity and being selfless. Or as Tony Robbins says, *the secret of living is giving.* That does not mean you put yourself last and ignore your needs and desires. On the contrary, you need to love yourself first in order to love others such as pampering yourself with a spa day, or a manicure when appropriate.

If you are in a less-than-optimal physical condition due to poor habits and poor choices, then a spa session may not be the best way to love yourself. Better habits with regard to diet and physical activity, and a friend to support you in your journey, would be a much better way to express love for yourself. Just like in finance, set goals and act on them to improve your situation. We have only one vehicle on this journey called life. True love and respect for yourself and your body, mental health, and financial state mean maintaining it at optimum functional capacity. You are responsible for your decisions that determine how you look and feel.

The most powerful words in the English language are "I AM." What you think of yourself is what you manifest. If you were told you are a failure, and you start to believe it, those words will shape how you feel about yourself and how you treat yourself and those around you. Loving yourself starts with creating boundaries with the people in your life and who respect them. It requires you to know yourself, your strengths and weaknesses, what you like, what makes you smile, and what makes you cry. The factors that change your state of mind, increase your energy, influence your decisions, and move you to action.

Let us celebrate love every day. Always be kind, forgiving, understanding, caring, respectful, and ready to help others. Loving yourself means growing and being strong because you did the hard things, asked for help when you needed it, and supported others when they needed it.

Today, I have carved out a good life. One where the struggles of the past only bolster my desire to help others. Coaching and telling my story at speaking engagements, bringing hope to those around me. But not just hope, I offer many ways to plan, strategize to be real, and keep your heart strong - a way to achieve and to live with passion and financial freedom!

Wishing everyone a happy joyful life filled with passion, love, and success and *Wealth IV Generations* to come.

References

1. Clark, C. (2025, March 26). *Here's the net worth you need in 2025 to rank in the top 25%, 10%, 0.1% of Americans — how do you stack up right now?* Moneywise. https://moneywise.com/managing-money/how-to-earn-money/heres-the-net-worth-you-need-in-2025-to-rank-in-the-top-25-10-01-of-americans

2. CNBC. (2018, September 13). *These retirement funds took a beating in 2008 — it could happen again.* https://www.cnbc.com/2018/09/13/these-retirement-funds-took-a-beating-in-2008-it-could-happen-again.html

3. CNBC. (2023, February 23). *401(k) retirement savings account balances sank in 2022, Fidelity says.* https://www.cnbc.com/2023/02/23/401k-retirement-savings-account-balances-sank-in-2022-fidelity-says.html

4. Kagan, J. (2025, January 26). *What is the Equal Credit Opportunity Act (ECOA)?* Investopedia. https://www.investopedia.com/terms/e/ecoa.asp

Erica Elliott

WarriorHeart Healing Hearts
Counselor, Brain Code Strategist, Speaker, and Author

https://www.linkedin.com/in/erica-elliott-ms-lpc-b90911150
https://www.facebook.com/warriorheartxo
https://www.instagram.com/warriorheartxo
https://msha.ke/warriorheartxohttps://linktr.ee/WarriorHeartxo

I possess a Master's Degree in Counseling Psychology and have invested over three decades in my career as a Licensed Counselor, Certified Brain Health Coach, and Certified Health Integrative Medicine Professional. My expertise encompasses a broad spectrum of therapeutic approaches, such as Neurobiology, ADHD and Neurodiversity, Somatic Therapy, Energy Medicine, NLP, CBT, RET, EFT, TFT, Theology, EMDR, the Gottman Method, alongside Mindfulness and Meditation. I am an international acclaimed author, speaker and spent over a decade in the military. I am the owner of WarriorHeart Healing Hearts. As a Brain Code Strategist I champion a comprehensive healing approach to harmonizes the mind, body, and spirit. I help individuals clear up the mess to discover their MASTERPIECE using a combination of healing modalities to rapidly rewire for success! Throughout my career, I've had the privilege of helping thousands of individuals, viewing my work not merely as a profession but as a calling. I am truly passionate about empowering others to grow, heal, and soar, unlocking the incredible life that God has always envisioned for them. Having navigated my own share of trials, traumas, and triggers, I deeply understand that healing flourishes through compassionate relationships. Together, we cultivate resilience and vitality, transforming legacies. Like iron sharpening iron, if you're looking for support or just want to connect, you were destined for greatness! Be Blessed and Be a Blessing!

A True Story of Healing, Hope, and a Faith-Led Reset After Long COVID

By Erica Elliott

It wasn't an ordinary day—it was a day that changed my life forever.

My husband had just come home from surgery after an altercation at work where he broke his leg taking a guy down in a scuffle. As a police officer, he'd encountered plenty of danger, but no one expects the hospital to be the greatest risk. Within 24 hours, he was sick with COVID and the flu, contracted from the hospital. He didn't fare well with having both and painkillers; he was a mess, so when I got sick, I didn't really pay attention to it. I needed to take care of him.

You see, the day he broke his leg was fueled with its own terrors. I got a call from our son saying he got a call that dad was shot, and did I know what was going on. Immediately running to the car to take off, speeding as fast as I could drive, heart pounding, shaking, thinking the worst since I couldn't get a hold of him or the department. Finally, I got one of the officers on the phone, saying he had been taken to the hospital by ambulance. It wasn't until I got closer to the hospital that I got a hold of one of the officers there with him at the hospital and found out he had broken his leg, not shot. Later, we found out that the guy he took down had shot a gun, but not at him; that's why they had taken him in. I got to the hospital, and my husband was pretty out of it from the meds they gave him. I told him the story of our son calling me and we thought he was shot. He then proceeded to tell me he thought he had died. His leg was broken behind him with the bone showing, and the ambulance driver gave him a shot that sent him looking almost catatonic, but he reported he thought he was dead and even remembers seeing over his body in the ambulance and thinking, well dang, how did I die from a broken leg. He said he could see the EMT behind him from above and his body below, and then said to himself, *"Well I guess at least I was on duty and my wife and kids will be taken care of.*" Then he said it was like the ambulance closed in on him, and he didn't remember anything else until he was at the hospital and they woke him. The EMT later said that he looked straight at him and said, "*Tell me the truth. Am I dead?*"

What a trip....

What a scare....

So, COVID seemed pale in comparison.

This was 2020. Fear and confusion were everywhere, but honestly, I wasn't that concerned at first. I rarely got sick. I was very active, exercised regularly, and even ran, health-conscious, prayed daily, and stayed in good shape. I had no idea what was on the other side of this, but I didn't think any of it was bad, just something we had to get through. My life was full—I worked for the federal government full-time, plus had a private counseling practice, and always had enough energy to go the extra mile. It was nothing for me to work 60 to 80 hours a week. Even in high school, I worked five jobs plus at least two all my life, except when my daughter was born until she graduated high school. I didn't slow down. That was just who I was.... Or at least, what I believed "Who I was".

But what started as fatigue and loss of taste and smell turned into something that knocked me off my feet and turned my world upside down, literally and figuratively.

I tried to press on. I had clients to care for. My family needed me. I've always been that "suck it up and drive on" kind of woman. Military-trained. Tough-minded. Spiritually rooted. I figured I'd outlast this like everything else.

Except I didn't.

Instead, things got worse. The headaches turned into days-long migraines. I felt bruised all over and electrical surges through my hands and feet. I couldn't walk to the mailbox without gasping for air, and there were many times I couldn't walk to the kitchen without severe pain. Chest pain gripped me—but I brushed it off, assuming it was related to my mitral valve prolapse and SVT. I even tried light workouts, only to crash harder. Still, I pushed.

And pushing broke me down further.

When I finally went to the doctor, the list of symptoms tumbled out: migraines, fatigue, shock-like pins and needle pains in my limbs, rashes, tinnitus, eye strain, headaches that never stopped, and chest pain. Bloodwork revealed hypothyroidism, adrenal fatigue, hyperkalemia, and my heart scans showed pericarditis plus bradycardia issues, POTS...my system was in distress. I kept trying to show up for my clients, often lying on the couch doing sessions by phone. But my mind wasn't working right. I'd lose words mid-sentence, and have problems with the right words; I had memory problems, I was stuttering, and I had panic attacks. I'd always been sharp. In fact, I had just applied for my doctorate a few months before. Now, I felt like a shadow of myself.

The deeper truth? I was scared. But I didn't let myself feel it at first. Because that would've meant stopping. Slowing down. Admitting I needed help. And I didn't know how to do that.

In the military, going to sick call—even for real issues—was often seen as malingering. That mentality had sunk in deep. I minimized my pain, even to myself. But slowly, everything inside me began to unravel. I felt misunderstood, even by doctors. Some didn't know what was going on, and no one knew what to do. They kept telling me that most people who have these kinds of symptoms get better in four to six months, and that I just needed to be patient. No one ever said it, but it made me feel like my symptoms were exaggerated, like it was psychosomatic or something. I withdrew from people—not because I didn't love them, but because I couldn't bear to explain what I didn't understand myself. Plus, we had been to a lot of funerals, three in a two-week time period of police officers, a few younger than me, who all died from COVID. Who was I to complain about this stuff? People were dying. As the months went on, the difficulty of dealing with this invisible disease that they could only call Post-Covid Syndrome began to wear even more on my psyche.

As a counselor for over 30 years, I had walked people through the darkest valleys. But now, I found myself in one, unsure of how to climb out.

One day, lying on the couch in so much pain with tears streaming down my face, I cried out to God, "I don't think I can do this the rest of my life."

That prayer wasn't a sweet prayer but a tearful, painful, prayer of desperation. I was tired of the pain. I was tired of not having answers. I was tired of hiding. I was so physically and mentally spent. I was afraid, and the months had now turned into almost a year.

God didn't shout or scold, but He was somewhat firm as if to say, "*I'm here...*" I heard a gentle but firm whisper: "*That's not what you told your daughter when she was going through her pain.*"

In that sacred moment, I remembered something profound. Years earlier, my daughter had said those same words to me—"*I can't go through this pain anymore*"—when she was battling a severe illness that almost cost her life. What did I do? I spoke life over her. I prayed. I reminded her of who she was and Whose she was. I helped her visualize her healing and speak God's word over her, bringing it into existence.

And now, God was asking me to do the same, reminding me also of the many people I have helped over the years out of their pain.

I began to see my healing journey through a new lens—not as a punishment or failure, but as an invitation to surrender.

And in surrender, I found power.

I reconnected to scriptures that had always carried me:

"I can do all things through Christ who gives me strength." – *Philippians 4:13 (NIV)*

But this time, I noticed something different. It didn't say "I can do all things through my effort" or "through my pushing." It was Christ's strength I needed. And I had been trying to do it all on my own.

Out of total surrender, I had to make one of the hardest choices, stepping away from my government job. It felt like failure at first. But deep down, I knew I couldn't keep pushing myself the way I had been and expect to heal. Something had to shift.

It wasn't easy. And it definitely wasn't overnight. But day by day, I started taking micro-steps—doing what I could, when I could, no matter how small. As I leaned into God, He began guiding me to use certain tools I had used with others and to new tools and treatments. I connected with Dr. Amen's clinic, started hyperbaric oxygen therapy at home, and slowly began seeing glimpses of improvement. A little more energy. A little more clarity. I could see a few clients again and start contributing in small ways.

Somewhere along the way, my body started responding. My brain began functioning more clearly. The debilitating symptoms started loosening their grip. I stopped trying to push through and started listening—really listening—to what my body needed. Rest. Nourishment. Grace. Some days I rested more than I worked.

That's when a new question arose: What do I truly want for my life moving forward?

If nothing stood in my way—no limitations, no illness—what kind of life would I create? I started revisiting how I used to partner with God's Word to manifest His best. I asked God to show me clearly: What patterns brought me here? Not to condemn myself, but to learn. What could I do differently now? What do I want my life to look like in a year from now and five years from now?

One thing was certain: I wasn't living. I had been surviving. And I was ready for more.

That's when something shifted.

It wasn't a perfect day. In fact, it was the opposite. I was still in the thick of it—two years post-COVID and still battling symptoms like brain fog, anxiety, fatigue, heart palpitations, myalgia, and panic attacks. Even with treatments, something inside still felt stuck. I needed joy. I needed movement. I needed connection.

I was seeing my own counselor and a coach, doing the internal work, but I also knew—I never wanted to end up this depleted again. I needed a spark.

So, I picked up the phone.

As a counselor of over 30 years and a brain health coach, I've helped thousands of people through trauma, grief, burnout, and more. I've studied neuroscience, natural medicine, and Scripture. But I've also learned this: Real healing doesn't just happen in therapy rooms. It happens in life. In connection. In laughter. In exploration.

That day, I felt a gentle prompt to call my daughter.

She was seven months pregnant, her husband was deployed, and I could hear the weariness in her voice. I said, "*Sweetie, I miss you. What if we made a plan to get out once a week? Something fun! We could pretend like it's a mini-vacation. We could film it too—maybe help others get out of their own rut.*"

She paused, then said, "*Actually... that sounds really good. And I could film content while we're out.*" She was hesitant to try new food places, but she said yes.

That one yes shifted everything.

Our first outing was to a peaceful coffee shop called *Selah*. It felt like a divine pause—chandeliers, soft music, and a calming atmosphere. We laughed, took pictures, and felt light again. Something lifted in both of us.

We started filming our adventures and created a social page called *Oklahoma HotSpots. One to two new places a week, nothing fancy, just us. But to our surprise, people responded. "Where is this?" "Thank you—this helped me get out of the house."* Then, business owners started asking how much we charged.

Wait—what?

We weren't charging anything. We were just healing and having fun. But doors opened. My daughter, finishing her marketing degree, saw the potential. We created packages, landed clients, and built a team. And yes—She became my boss, and I loved watching her shine.

We built something beautiful—out of burnout, out of isolation, out of nothing but willingness to step out and have fun.

This wasn't just about coffee shop pictures. I've worked with people stuck in trauma cycles: wake up, stay inside, go to bed, repeat. It's not living, it's surviving. And when the brain associates safety with solitude, it makes even joy feel unsafe.

But there's a reason Jesus sent the disciples out two by two. Healing happens in connection.

Our weekly outings became therapy. They gave us joy, purpose, laughter—and they empowered others too. One woman messaged saying she hadn't gone out since COVID, but after our videos, she did. Another man started weekly outings with his mom.

That's when we realized—this wasn't just a hobby. It was ministry.

And we were healing together.

My daughter, an empath and introvert, needed this joy as much as I did. We dreamed again. Laughed again. Rediscovered life again. We met inspiring business owners with stories of faith and resilience. It was holy ground.

The business thrived. And then came another unexpected invitation.

My husband decided to retire. One day, he said, *"What if we sold everything, bought a yacht, and did The Great Loop?"* At first, I hesitated. I still didn't feel 100%. But the more we prayed and talked, the more peace we felt. Life is precious. Too many never get the chance to live their dream.

So, we said yes. We sold almost everything. Bought the boat. Traveled from Kemah, Texas, to three-fourths of Florida and eight amazing islands of the Bahamas. You can find some of our journey on our YouTube channel, *WarriorHeart Travels*. We became debt-free, built our dream home, and discovered what true wealth really looks like—abundance that doesn't come at the cost of your health.

And during that season, something else was born.

I finally began writing the book God had laid on my heart for years. *Breath of Heaven: Manifesting God's Way* began to take shape—anchored in biblical truth and brain science, and filled with the steps I personally used that God has taught me over the years to go from fear and fatigue, to peace and purpose. It's for anyone who feels stuck in survival mode. Anyone who's tired, uncertain, or holding on by a thread. I wrote it for you.

Maybe you've been in that place where you don't know if you can go on... or even dream again. Let me speak life to you:

You are not stuck. You are not too far gone. You are not too old, too tired, too sick, or too late.

All it takes is one brave step. One phone call. One outing. One yes.

You never know what God might do with your willingness.

Your miracle might just be waiting outside your front door. Go create a life you love—you never know how beautiful it can become.

Through out my journey I have learned a lot and here are the 7 steps God walked me through—biblical, neurological, and personal practices that created freedom and clarity from the inside out. These aren't theories. They are lived truths. They're the process of becoming who God designed you to be.

Step 1: Pause and Breathe

In the early stages of my post-COVID healing, there were days when the only thing I could manage was to breathe. And honestly, even that felt like a battle. I would place my hand over my heart, close my eyes, and whisper, "*God, please help me inhale peace and healing and exhale saying I release fear.*" I had been trained to be strong, to "suck it up and drive on," as we say in the military. But what I had to learn in this season was that strength sometimes looks like softness—like surrendering to the present moment and breathing it in. Like tuning into what I need in this moment. This was the time I really leaned more into meditation.

Breathing isn't just relaxation—it's neurological reprogramming. When we breathe slowly and intentionally, we send a message to the brain that we are safe. And when the brain feels safe, it opens up to healing and insight. Meditation with breath can help our bodies sink into a deeper healing state.

Breathing isn't a small thing. It's the foundation. It's the way we pause the chaos and invite heaven in. And sometimes, when that's all you can do—it's more than enough to begin your journey to freedom.

Step 2: Notice the Program

It's hard to heal what you don't even know is there. I remember one day, after weeks of feeling like I was making no progress, I found myself crying on the couch again. I had been doing "all the right things," but still felt stuck and so angry at my body for failing me. That's when God dropped a gentle truth into my spirit: *"You're still running old programs."* That phrase hit me like a wave. If I really wanted something different, I had to find all the old programs and clear them up. I also had to get really clear on what I wanted in my life to rewire a new program.

So much of what we do, think, feel, and believe is not conscious. It's patterned. It's programmed. It's rehearsed behavior and belief that was wired into us in childhood, trauma, culture, experience, or even the lies we tell ourselves. And until we notice the program, we'll keep repeating it.

You don't have to be controlled by old programming. But you do have to see it first. Awareness is the first miracle.

Step 3: Speak What You Seek

I'll never forget the day I heard myself say, *"I'm so tired of being stuck."* And instantly, I felt the Holy Spirit say back, *"Then stop reinforcing that narrative with your words."* Whoa! That one moment shifted everything. I tell clients this all of the time, *"You have to speak what you want over your life."*

Our words are not just sounds. They're seeds. They plant into our subconscious and into the spiritual realm. They give our minds—and our miracles—directions to follow.

Your voice is a spiritual and neurological weapon. Speak as if it's already done. Because in the kingdom—it is.

Step 4: Visualize the Victory

Before I ever stood on stage, wrote a book, built a business, or even walked into healing, I saw it in my mind and felt it in my soul. I would close my eyes, not to escape—but to prepare. I imagined myself whole, vibrant, focused, even joyful. I saw myself helping others. I envisioned rooms filled with love, joy, and light. I pictured freedom—and it became a seed of faith inside me. This is actually a tool I learned when I was a young girl. When I was about 12 or 13, after reading the Bible out of desperation, God led me to read a book called "The Power of Positive Thinking" by Norman Vincent Peale. I began using this tool every night with all the things that I wanted to happen in my life, honestly, to escape the hell I was in as a hope for something better. Every one of those things came true except for one, and that one was one of those things that I would say sometimes, "I thank God for the unanswered prayers," as the song by Garth Brooks goes.

See it until you believe it. See it until you become it. Move like it's already who you are and what you want.

Step 5: Feel It Fully

There's a sacred moment that happens when you stop running from your emotions and finally sit down with them. For me, it happened late one night, in the quiet, no distractions—just the ache in my chest, and the truth I couldn't outrun. A reminding of what I took clients through, not pushing emotions away, but feeling them and letting them pass to release them from the body and mind differently. I had to feel the grief. The fear. The loss. I had to feel it in order to heal it. Even the Word of God shows Jesus having lots of different emotions.

Your emotions are not the enemy. They're invitations to healing.

Once you release them, your emotions can be a guidance system, like a GPS, helping you notice when you are on track or off track towards what you want and what serves you better in life.

You can then learn to tune into your emotions when you feel peace then you are on track. When you feel something is off or feels negative, tune release the emotion, and then ask what would be better in this moment or what is the next step for me to take.

Step 6: Rewire with Repetition

Rewiring doesn't happen in a day or a week. It happens daily. For me, it was declaring scripture over my life when I didn't feel it. It was praying when I was tired. It was doing breathwork and neuropsych tools that I taught when my emotions were all over the place. It was asking myself if what I was doing was moving me closer or away from what I said I really wanted in my life. Healing came in layers—through repetition.

Consistency creates clarity. And clarity rewires destiny.

Step 7: Act in Alignment

Selling everything and starting over wasn't easy, but it was freeing and sinking into bravery to the unknown—it was also obedience. Obedience to what we felt called to. We didn't have a perfect plan. We had a prompting. And every time we said yes, God met us with provision, guidance, and miracles. Alignment is not just what you believe—it's what you "do" in response to belief.

Faith is not passive. It's progressive. And the more you act on truth, and stay true to your course, the more it becomes your new normal.

I pray this book has blessed you and that you use and share the tools you've learned. I have a book that expands these areas and so much more that will be released on November of 2025 called **"Brain Coding - *We Repeat What We Don't Rewire – It's a Program.*"** This book will walk you through the deeper science of your thought patterns, habits, emotional coding, and how to build a daily system to live in the fullness of God's design.

If you found this book helpful, may I ask you a favor to please leave a review on Amazon. Thank you!

As a Brain Code Strategist, I help people rewire with evidence-based tools to rapidly clear the mess and transform your life into the successful Masterpiece you were always created to be! People also love me speaking to their groups and organizations, teaching them tools in a fun, interactive, and transformative way. Excited to connect with you and please find free resources on the link below. I am always adding new tools and links. Be Blessed and Be a Blessing!

Sylvia Becker-Hill

Becker-Hill Inc.

https://www.linkedin.com/in/sylviabeckerhill/
https://www.facebook.com/sylvia.beckerhill/
https://www.instagram.com/sylviabeckerhill/
https://becker-hill.com/
https://sylviabecker-hill.com

Sylvia Becker-Hill is a trailblazing Renaissance Woman and the creator of the Neuro Creativity™ framework, where applied neuroscience, somatic coaching, intentional creativity, and energy management converge. Since 1997, she has empowered thousands of executives, women leaders, and entrepreneurs worldwide to break free from outdated paradigms and design lives of impact and joy. In 2002, Sylvia became the first German coach to earn the coveted Professional Certified Coach designation from the International Coach Federation, and in 2023 she was named one of the world's first ten Certified Master Neuroplasticians—a recognition of her expertise in rewiring the brain for lasting transformation. A multiple international bestselling author and seasoned edutainer, she blends science, soul, and artistry into experiences that spark profound personal transformation. Her mission is clear: to help you "FLIP" everything that blocks, hurts, or sabotages you into unquestionable Freedom, unconditional Love, envisioned Identity, and impactful Power

FLIP Waiting to Creating:
The Quantum Practice of Gratitude

By Sylvia Becker-Hill

"Gratitude is the best attitude."
~Maya Angelou

My Gratitude Epiphany

Have you ever found yourself sitting in a beautiful place, surrounded by what "should" feel good—and yet, your body feels numb, heavy, or just... off?

It happened to me one sunny afternoon in Southern California a few years ago. I had a healthy lunch at Swamie's in Carlsbad on the iconic Highway 101, an inspiring conversation with a dear Irish wise girlfriend. A perfect summer day outdoors in my garden, which every visitor simply called "paradise".

But when I scanned my body, I felt no joy. No gratitude. Just a dull ache behind my eyes and the mental noise of a to-do list whispering, *"You're behind again." "You have not finished this morning what you promised yourself to be done with 3 weeks ago!" "How long will you keep procrastinating?"*

In that moment, I realized something essential: **I was waiting for gratitude to happen to me.**

I had made the experience of gratitude conditional!

I had lived with unconscious beliefs that held a clear logic:

When X finally happens, THEN I have the permission to feel grateful.

Like most people, I was trained to feel grateful "because of" something—a gift, a success, a kind gesture. That's the **classic Newtonian model**: life acts on us, and we react with emotion. But what if that's not the only way? **What if gratitude could begin in the body—not in reaction, but in creation?**

What if you could FLIP the order?

The Default Model:
Newton's Trap of Reaction-Based Gratitude

"Be grateful you have any food at all on your plate!
Think of the poor starving children in Africa!
They would be grateful if they had what you have."
~My Grandmother

My grandparents looked after me when my parents were at work. My grandmother was a loving, kind, yet also bitter, withering woman. She had lost her home in the far east of the German Reich and the life she had built to the Russian invasion during WWII. She had been with my grandfather, mother, and uncle refugees for two years to escape the Russian soldiers' killing and raping. They had starved for nearly four years. She had been a devoted Roman Catholic Christian, praying daily. I think she felt abandoned by God. A bit like Jesus, who supposedly said during his torturous hours hanging on the cross: "Father, father, why have you forsaken me?"

In the house I later grew up in with her, she had Jesus on big crosses hanging in every room. His naked, exposed body, blood dripping realistically painted from several wounds, and the thorny crown on his head looked down on my toddler self. His eyes felt like following me around, checking if I was a "good girl."

When I pulled a face or made a pout because what she cooked looked strange, or when I didn't like the taste, my grandmother ALWAYS sternly reprimanded me with the "starving children in Africa". Then, she looked up at Jesus and rolled her eyes. I was a child. I didn't even know where Africa was, nor that African children had dark skin. I only learned "*I am at fault, a sinner.*" "*I should be grateful.*" **Gratitude became meshed up with guilt and shame.**

In school, I got trained to say "thank you" after adults spoke to me or gave me something. Gratitude became a polite "reaction"—a **social reflex** following a favorable event. You get the job? Be grateful. Your partner surprises you with flowers? Be grateful. You have your health? Be grateful.

All lovely ideas—but they reinforce one assumption: **Gratitude is a response to life, not a creator of it.**

This is the emotional inheritance of the Newtonian worldview. It sees the universe as a machine: cause → effect. Something happens in the world; you respond in your nervous system. Trigger leads to emotion. External precedes internal. Matter precedes energy.

It's linear. Predictable. And **deeply disempowering**.

Why? Because it makes your inner state and how you feel conditioned to external events that are most of the time outside your control!

Even worse: What happens when life throws you challenge after challenge? When you're grieving, feel anxious, or are burned out? Gratitude feels impossible in these situations. Inaccessible. Almost offensive, as if you were spiritually bypassing your emotional truth.

But here's the shift that changes everything: Gratitude doesn't have to be earned! It can be **chosen.**

The Quantum Model: Choosing to Feel First

"I experience a sexually fulfilled, emotionally evolved,
and spiritually inspired partnership in which my partner and
I support each other to grow into our highest possibilities."
~Sylvia Becker-Hill, January 2000,
embodying her future marriage

Welcome to the FLIP.

As I began to embrace gratitude as a choice, I realized that it wasn't just a mindset shift—it was a fundamental reimagining of how I related to the world.

Quantum physics teaches us that **energy precedes matter**. That potential exists before it collapses into form. In this paradigm, emotions are not passive outcomes but "active ingredients." When we embody gratitude before there's a "reason" to feel it, **we're not faking—it, we're "activating" a new emotional reality sensed and felt in our body.**

There is a meme circulating online that claims that the brain doesn't distinguish between an imagined experience and a real one. That is a false generalization! Real data coming in through external or internal receptors generally gets recognized as real, while the weaker, imagined image gets recognized as imagined. **When imagination is vivid and carries a strong positive or negative charge, THEN the brain's reality threshold gets confused and takes the imagined image for REAL!**

That means, when you "choose" to feel grateful by putting all your attention fully and intentionally on it somatically, **you create gratitude out of nothing**—and your creation rewires your neural pathways! Your body begins to believe and behave as if what you want is already here. That's not denial. That's creation.

As a practicing Certified Master Neuroplastician, I've seen this shift in my clients: They stop waiting. They start creating. And the results are stunning!

One of my female executive clients dreamed of becoming CEO in a different company from the one she was working for. After I showed her how to create the sensations of gratitude in her body, she relived it every day as a morning ritual for a few weeks, and a headhunter reached out to her 'out of the blue' through LinkedIn, inviting her to apply for a CEO position in her industry. Her example validated the generative power of gratitude!

This is also how I created, after two failed engagements surrounded at the time by social circles filled with cynicism about love and marriage, my bliss-filled, beautiful partnership with my husband from the opposite side of the world for the last 25 years, and still going strong! I created all - not just gratitude - embodied sensation of my vision of my desired partnership to such a **vivid level of clarity in my body that there was no space left for doubt or fear.**

This is the first meaning of **FLIP**: More **F**reedom, more **L**ove, **I**dentity curation, and the **P**ower to create results and impact. These are the embodied outcomes when a woman stops reacting to life and begins shaping it from within. This is my superpower behind my beautiful life. People often ask me, *"Wow, Sylvia, how did you create all THIS?"*

Now you know!

Somatics: The Body as the Stage of Emotion

"My parents told me every day that they loved me.
Yet, being traumatized during World War II,
they were subconsciously stuck in fear.
While my brain heard "love," my body sensed "danger".
That conditioned me to a lifetime of hypervigilance that felt normal
and made me addicted to adrenaline, sugar, and stress."
~Sylvia Becker-Hill

Gratitude isn't just a thought. It's a "felt state."

You can read affirmations all day long, but if your body doesn't follow, the change doesn't stick. That's why my work centers on "somatics"— the study and practice of experiencing the body from within.

We all have three sensory channels:

- **Exteroception**: what we feel from the outside world through our five+ senses (light, sound, temperature).
- **Proprioception**: the awareness of our body in space, balance, and gravity.
- **Interoception**: the inward sensing of our own inner world (heartbeat, breath, warmth, tightness, etc.), which is crucial for the skills I'm teaching!

Gratitude, when practiced somatically, becomes a full-body sensation. Warmth in the chest. A softening behind the eyes. Spacious breath. It activates your parasympathetic nervous system, lowers cortisol, and builds emotional resilience.

Polyvagal Theory, developed by Dr. Stephen Porges, explains how our autonomic nervous system shifts between safety and threat responses. Gratitude—especially felt in the body—helps us move into a "ventral vagal" state: calm, connected, creative.

Your body "wants" to feel safe. Yet when your nervous system is stuck in survival, it needs more than information. It needs to experience over and over again a new pattern of cues of safety. Once you can finally relax because your body feels safe, creating gratitude becomes as natural as breathing in and out.

After I nearly died from decades of depleting my adrenal glands and my body breaking down under the constant onslaught of stress hormones and I ended up first in the ER twice, and then incapable of working for many months in retreat at home, I studied, learned, got certified in somatic coaching and implemented daily nervous system regulation processes, movements, energy management, grounding, earthing, soothing... **I finally started to feel safe within my own body and the world!**

I finally could sense how the temptation of the allure of excitement didn't serve me.

I finally learned to set boundaries and became immune to FOMO, the fear of missing out, and enjoyed a less busy, less hustling, deeper, and joy-filled lifestyle.

A new way of living crystallized in which gratitude became completely unconditional and a daily conscious choice.

The FLIP Practice: How to Feel Gratitude First

"You've always had the power, my dear,
you just had to learn it for yourself."
~Glinda, the Good Witch in the Wizard of Oz 1939

So how do we practice FLIPPING the order?

We start with the second layer of the FLIP acronym—how we do the work:

Fun, **L**ightness, **I**magination, **P**lay.

Gratitude becomes easier when we **drop the "adulting" performance and invite in curiosity.** Playfulness isn't frivolous. It's essential. It rewires trauma.

It reconnects us to the **Inner Child** who once laughed just because sunlight danced on a puddle. I bought myself a mermaid Barbie in my 50s, just because I never had one as a girl. I bought bubble gum and trained for days how to chew it and blow the air into it to make big bubbles. I blow soap bubbles as often as I can because they make my inner child giggle. I now have a conscious, daily active relationship with my inner child, and spaces in our house and garden are tangibly and visibly dedicated to it. My art studio is, for example, in a former children's playhouse with shutters that have heart-shaped cut-outs under the shady protection of my peppertree.

Here is a simple FLIP Practice:

Freedom – Ask: *"What thought or weight can I release in this moment?"*

Love – Breathe love into your heart, breathe out any resistance and judgments. Recall a person or pet who makes you smile.

Identity – Curate yourself: *"I am someone who creates beauty."*

Power – Choose: *"How can I create impact today, from this state?"*

I had countless coaches, mentors, and Law of Attraction experts preaching to me the "power of gratitude" by asking me: *"What are you grateful for in your life right now?"* They had good intentions, yet **they were unaware of how disempowering that question is!** The way they asked that question - and many coaches, therapists, and Law of Attraction experts still do! - is stuck in the Newtonian World model and makes gratitude conditional and attached to results that must have already happened! I agree. Their question is better than asking their clients to focus on what is lacking in their life, but why not ask more empowering questions like these:

- "What do you need to allow yourself to experience gratitude right now in your body?"
- "How does embodying gratitude feel in your body? Sense its cues and describe them out loud!"
- "What small, simple movement - like clapping your hands with glee - or action - like jumping up and down - might help you to intensify that beautiful feeling of gratitude even more right now?"

And now the how:

Fun – Put on music. Move. Dance for 90 seconds.

Lightness – Smile. Even if you don't feel it yet. Let the face lead the body.

Imagination – Picture your future self thanking you for today's shift.

Play – Write a gratitude letter from your 90-year-old self to your current one. Make it poetic. Make it silly. Just make it yours.

My favorite personal way of FLIPing myself in any moment into a productive, creative state from which I can choose to embody anything I want is - drum rolls - **Doodling!!!** Yes, you read that correctly: Doodling. I set my timer on my phone for 60 seconds (On bad days for 3 minutes). I put a pen in the middle of a blank piece of paper and **INTENTIONALLY, without controlling** the movement of my hand (!) I allow the pen to dance over the paper. Intentionally means I hold one focus, for example "clarity", or a specific question, or "I need an idea for XYZ." After the alarm goes off, I write down what comes to my mind through the activation of my brain. It is often magical and powerful!

This is how you stop waiting to feel good. You become the cause.

You become a "**Neuro-Artist of Gratitude**"!

Resistance and Real Talk:
When Life Feels Too Hard to Feel Grateful

"Embodiment is protection against bypassing."
~Sylvia Becker-Hill

Now, let me be honest.

Some days, shifting ourselves into authentic gratitude feels impossible. Grief, trauma, and burnout create a kind of neurological fog that gratitude can't always pierce immediately. I'm not here to tell you to "just be grateful" when your world feels like it's falling apart.

But I am here to say: **Even in darkness, a micro-shift is possible!**

Try this: Find one neutral sensation. Your feet on the ground. The softness of a blanket. The temperature of the air. Stay with it. Let your body anchor into it now. That's the doorway. Not a bypass. A bridge.

This is not about toxic positivity. It's about somatic possibility.

Gratitude is not just a state you enter when life is good. It's a muscle you train so that when life gets hard, you have emotional strength already built.

Five Misconceptions About Gratitude

"You don't have to wait for life to be perfect.
You get to feel grateful now."
~Sylvia Becker-Hill

Let's dismantle some myths that keep people stuck and suspicious of gratitude. These misconceptions are usually rooted in a mechanical, Newtonian view of the world—where cause and effect must be linear, where results must be visible before belief is allowed, and where emotions are treated as side effects rather than creative forces.

Here are five of the most common blocks:

1. "I need to feel good before I can feel grateful."

True gratitude is *generative*, not reactive. It's not only a trained response to things going well. It's a *choice* to open the heart, and that choice can shift the entire field of your experience.

2. "If I'm grateful, I can't be angry or sad."

Gratitude is not a competitor emotion—it's a companion. You can hold both: gratitude and grief, gratitude and anger, gratitude and confusion. The ability to hold both is a sign of maturity, not contradiction.

3. "Gratitude means I'm okay with how things are."

Gratitude doesn't mean settling. It means accessing your power *while* you create change. It means appreciating life *as it is* without giving up on what it could be.

4. "Gratitude is spiritual bypassing."

It can be—if it's forced or fake. But authentic gratitude is deeply embodied. It makes room for discomfort. It doesn't cover pain; it creates a wider context around it. Real gratitude deepens your capacity to stay present.

5. "It's naive or delusional to feel grateful right now."

We live in a culture where skepticism is rewarded and emotional neutrality is treated as maturity. But what if clarity, not cynicism, is the true maturity? What if the courage to feel grateful *without needing proof* is the mark of leadership?

These myths collapse the moment you experience what real, grounded, embodied gratitude feels like. And once you do, it's not just a nice idea. It's a new baseline.

That's the **secret.** That's the **rebellion.** And that's where **real transformation** begins.

Gratitude, Leadership, and Rebellion

"In a world addicted to outrage, feeling grateful is radical."
~Sylvia Becker-Hill

We're living in a time where fear sells headlines, where panic is monetized, and where cynicism is mistaken for intelligence. When everything around us seems to scream "Brace yourself," choosing to soften, to notice beauty, to feel gratitude—it isn't weakness.

It's rebellion.

To be grateful in a world that constantly tries to push you into fight-or-flight is to reclaim your **sovereignty.** You are saying: "I choose how I feel. I choose what I amplify. I choose what lives in my body."

Gratitude doesn't require denial. It requires discernment. It's not about ignoring the suffering or injustice. It's about choosing not to be *owned* by it. **It's an act of emotional self-governance in a world built to keep you emotionally hijacked.**

Gratitude is how you stay human. It's how you stay creative. It's how you remain a leader in your own life when everything around you tries to convince you you're a victim of chaos.

Becoming a Source of Gratitude

"Declaring out loud 'I am the source of everything I am experiencing' AND sensing the truth of that statement in my whole body was the moment of ultimate empowerment!"
~Sylvia Becker-Hill

You don't need to wait for life to give you a reason.
You are the reason.
You are the moment.
You are the artist.

To FLIP the order is to reclaim your sovereignty over your inner state. To choose gratitude first is to sculpt a reality from the inside out. Not with denial, but with devotion.

Gratitude is not a thank-you card to life. It's a tuning fork to your future.

So breathe into your body now.

Name one thing you're grateful for—not because it happened, but because you *choose* to feel it.

Then... smile.

You've just FLIPPED the order. You turned the vertically standing hourglass into an eternal-eight horizontal one that radiates goodness in all directions!

I love hearing from you, my dear readers: sylvia@becker-hill.com

Put the word GRATITUDE into the subject line and I'll respond personally!

xoxo,

Sylvia

Glossary of Key Terms and Concepts

Term	Definition
Affirmation	A positive statement repeated to influence your mindset or belief. Often used cognitively, but less effective without somatic integration.
Exteroception	The sensing of external stimuli (e.g., sight, sound, temperature) by the nervous system.
FLIP	A transformational acronym with two layers: (1) Freedom, Love, Identity curation, Power to create results and impact; (2) Fun, Lightness, Imagination, Play. It reflects both the outcomes and the methodology of somatic transformation.
Gratitude (Somatic)	A full-body experience of appreciation that includes emotional, physiological, and neurological activation—not just mental recognition.
Hebb's Law	A neuroscience principle: "Neurons that fire together wire together." Repetition strengthens neural pathways!
Inner Child	A psychological concept referring to the vulnerable, creative, and emotional part of the self formed in early life. Often engaged in healing and play-based practices.
Interoception	The internal sensing of bodily states (e.g., heart rate, breath, hunger), critical to emotional self-awareness and self-regulation.

Neuroplasticity	The brain's ability to change and rewire itself through experience, learning, and deliberate emotional states.
Newtonian Model	A linear, mechanistic view of cause and effect—used here to describe how emotions are often seen as reactions to external events.
Polyvagal Theory	A theory of the nervous system developed by Stephen Porges that explains how our physiological state (safety, threat) shapes behavior, connection, and emotion.
Quantum Model	A paradigm drawn from quantum physics suggesting that consciousness and energy precede physical outcomes. Applied here to emotional creation.
Somatics	The field of body-based awareness and transformation. In this context, it refers to generating emotional states through felt experience, not just thought.

Cyndee Paulson-Heer

Founder and CEO of The Sass n' Soul Life &
The Sass n' Soul Network

http://www.cyndeepaulsonheer.com
https://thesassnsoullife.com/
https://www.instagram.com/cyndeepaulsonheer/
https://www.linkedin.com/in/cyndeepaulsonheer/
https://www.facebook.com/cyndee.paulsonheer/
https://www.instagram.com/the_sass_n_soul_life/
https://www.facebook.com/TheSassNSoulLife/

Cyndee Paulson-Heer is the founder of *The Sass n' Soul Life, Sass n' Soul Network, and Sass n' Soul Magazine*. Through these platforms, she helps women live authentically, lead with purpose, and live their legacy of impact. An award-winning writer and speaker, she combines personal narrative with practical tools to guide women in breaking free from unconscious patterns and charting lives of meaning and contribution.

Her most defining life moment came one quiet morning at her desk, coffee in hand and children nearby. While drafting a psychology essay on parenting, as the endless bickering of her two oldest filled the room, she suddenly saw how her unexamined patterns would become their "inheritance." Looking into her youngest son's big blue eyes, she recalls: *"I saw my children's future staring back at me. The awareness hit me like a stone dropped in still water, rippling out the truth: if I did not crack the code of my own life and model the person I wanted them to become, I would pass down my unconscious patterns like family heirlooms—and my past would become their future."*

Standing at that crossroads, she chose not to drift but to drive—and that decision became the foundation of her life's work.

Today, through books, journals, her magazine, and her vibrant Sass n' Soul community, Cyndee helps women discover their voice, align with their values, and live by conscious choice. She is currently expanding her reach with collaborative anthologies and the ***Coffee Time with Cyndee* podcast**—platforms that celebrate authentic stories, lifelong learning, and women leading with vision and volition.

Drift or Drive:
Cancel Autopilot and Design a Life on Purpose

By Cyndee Paulson-Heer

The Real Assignment

I've always been an early riser. There's something about the quiet before the world wakes up that feels like possibility. That morning was no different—coffee in hand, sunlight beaming in through the blinds, with me sitting at my desk. I was working on a psychology assignment: an essay on parenting, when my youngest, 2 1/2 years of age, toddled over to me and asked something. For the life of me, I can't recall what it was.

Across the room, his older siblings—twelve and fifteen—were at it again. Their endless sibling "dance" of bickering filled the air, a soundtrack to which I had grown almost numb.

It should have been an ordinary morning. But something about that convergence—the words I was writing, the dull acceptance of their fighting, and the quiet steadiness in my toddler's eyes—caused something inside me to shift.

In a flash, I saw their future staring back at me. And the awareness hit me like a stone dropped in still water, rippling out the truth: *If I don't crack the code of my own life, I'll pass down my unconscious patterns like family heirlooms, and my past will become their future.*

That was my wake-up call: Continue on this trajectory of survival and dysfunction or step up to the wheel, even without all the answers, and chart a new course. With that, I closed the cover on the past and tapped my metaphoric white cane into the unknown . . .

Why a Life by Design Matters

There was no short supply of love in my dysfunctional family of origin, but I didn't come into adulthood with a sturdy foundation. Far from it. With a rage-aholic dad at the helm and a passive-aggressive mom navigating through lies, manipulation, and gaslighting, I grew up with mixed messages and no bedrock—no clear values, no steady compass. My dad could go from easy laughter to sharp anger in a heartbeat. One moment we were joking around, and the next, angry words and threats were flying before I could catch my breath. My mom, on the other hand, often expressed frustration sideways. Instead of simply asking me to clean the kitchen, she'd slam cabinet doors and clatter dishes into place. If I asked, "*What's wrong?*" the answer came clipped: *Nothing.*

She didn't always sidestep tension; sometimes she pushed back, provoking my dad when silence might have kept the peace. As children we hated sitting in the crossfire, but looking back, I understand why she did it. She had her own truth to speak, but without the tools to communicate directly, it came out sharp and sideways.

Those patterns seeped into me, shaping the way I learned to read a room, anticipate moods, and decide when to speak or stay silent. And in my own unconscious years of default, I mirrored them—I slammed cabinet doors, gave cold shoulders, and answered Nothing when everything inside me screamed otherwise. Those behaviors became part of my default programming.

But default doesn't have to be destiny. True story!

The moment you realize you have a choice—to keep replaying what you inherited or to design something new—is the moment everything begins to shift. That's when survival patterns lose their grip and the real work of becoming the next best version of yourself begins.

I do not want to villainize my parents. Like most people, they were a blend of good and bad. They did the best they could with the tools they had—carrying their own unhealed wounds into the way they parented and lived. Still, they were incredibly supportive of their children and our dreams. There was laughter in our home, and overall, they were good parents. My dad was the quintessential '50s tough guy, and my mom—straight A's and valedictorian—brought her own brand of drive and expectation to parenting.

She was a paradox I still carry with me. On the surface, she sometimes tiptoed around conflict, but beneath it, she was philanthropic, giving, and strong to her core—a force when she caught a vision of good and set her mind on bringing it to life. And she did it while raising four kids in the thick of the 1950s and 1960s, a man's world that gave women little room to rise. Yet rise she did. And watching her taught me, long before I had words for it, that contribution matters—that lives ripple when we dare to give, even in the face of resistance. That was her living legacy, which became part of mine.

But legacy alone wasn't enough to steady me. I had no map, no compass. I drifted. When push came to shove and I didn't know the way forward, I defaulted to the patterns I swore I wouldn't pass down—little passive-aggressive tantrums, sideways frustration.

A wake-up call shakes us for a reason: It's life tapping us on the shoulder and asking, *Are you awake, or are you drifting?*

Default: The Drift of Autopilot

Every one of us is already weaving a legacy. The question is: Are we doing it by default or by design?

By default, we hand down unexamined patterns, recycled fears, and unhealed wounds. Default may show up in sharp words under pressure, in choosing silence when we should speak, in biases we never examined. It feels familiar—safe even—but it doesn't ask us to grow. It doesn't invite us to wake up. Autopilot never takes us anywhere new; it just circles us in stagnant waters until unconscious loops harden into habits, shaping a legacy we never meant to leave.

Design: The Courage of Authorship

Design, by contrast, is authorship. It's taking hold of the pen and writing the story yourself—not just the chapters yet to come, but also rewriting the ones you inherited. Design is living on purpose—evaluating your beliefs, naming your values, aligning with your passions, and understanding what drives you and why. It's the conscious choice to stop reciting the script you never wrote and begin drafting one that reflects who you truly are and who you're becoming.

It's an ongoing conversation with yourself: *Who am I? Who am I not? Who do I want to become? What gap must I bridge?* It's waking up to the ripple effect of your actions—how they shape not just your life, but the lives of those you touch.

Where drifting dulls us, design awakens us. Where autopilot confines, authorship liberates. And design doesn't wait for "someday." It's lived in today's messy, imperfect choices that steadily shape your character, your journey, and your legacy over time.

The Real Question

It's never a matter of *whether* you will contribute—you always do. The real question is: What kind of contribution will you make? Will it be the unconscious drift of default, or the deliberate authorship of a life lived on purpose?

Alignment Check

- What unconscious patterns am I living or passing down?
- Are my steps moving me toward the story I want to live and leave?
- Am I drifting... or designing?

The Compass – Values (What Grounds You)

To move in the right direction, every traveler needs a compass. Without one, it's easy to confuse motion with momentum. You may feel busy, even productive, but without true orientation you can end up circling the same terrain.

A compass won't clear the fog, calm the storm, or pave the road ahead. But it will point true. It offers a steady nudge—a quiet, consistent signal to course-correct and guide you forward. Think of Rudolph's glowing nose or Ding-A-Ling's off-pitch bell: small, humble signals that, in the blinding storm, guided Santa home. They didn't remove the storm; they simply gave him something trustworthy to follow.

Storms will come. They may wash out the path, reroute your plans, or force you to pause. But uncertainty isn't the enemy—it's part of the terrain of becoming. When you are rooted in values deeper than circumstance, you don't need to see every step. You only need to trust the direction. And often, delays and detours are the universe nudging us back into alignment—just sayin'!

We all have values. But too often, they aren't hand-picked with conscious awareness—they're unconscious hand-me-downs. *Work hard. Don't rock the boat. Keep everyone happy.* Sound familiar? Political, religious, and cultural beliefs often slip in unnoticed, stamping themselves into the fabric of our being before we ever have the chance to ask: *Do I really believe this?* Left unchallenged, these borrowed values become the silent compass of our lives, pointing us toward destinations we may never have chosen.

My own reckoning was not gentle. It pulled me through every corner of life, forcing me to question everything—from what love really is to why I am here. It pressed me to look at all my roles: human, woman, mother, wife, friend. With each one, I had to ask: *What does this really mean to me?*

I realized that often times I wasn't navigating with my own compass. The needle was off. The map didn't match. Some borrowed values had set up residency for so long that they required eviction notices. So I picked up a demolition hammer and went to work. I tore down entire rooms I'd unconsciously built, allowing space so I could rebuild, retrofit with insight, and calibrate my compass to my True North—charting a map that was finally mine.

That journey eventually led me to the most essential question of all: *Are we innately good, or innately bad?* It became my fixed compass point, the question beneath every other question. And once I discovered my answer, the direction of my life changed.

You don't have to know the entire way forward—the way will show you the way.

Alignment Check

- Write down your top three values.
- Ask yourself: Where did these come from? Are they truly mine—or handed to me without question?
- Notice where they show up in your daily steps, and where they don't. Note what and where you can course correct, and make small shifts to align more completely.

The Map – Your Big Picture (and the GPS of Purpose)

A compass can tell you where North is, but it can't show you the land. For that, you need a map.

The map is your big picture. It reveals the lay of the land and the possible routes through it—the mountains you'll need to climb, the valleys you'll cross, the rivers you'll ford. It shows destinations and detours, alternate routes, landmarks that help you orient, and uncharted regions still waiting to be explored. But without direction, it's just terrain, just options. To navigate it, you need something more.

That's where purpose comes in. Purpose is your GPS. It doesn't erase the obstacles or smooth the terrain. It aligns you with your compass and helps you choose your route. When the trail gets rough, purpose steadies you. It drives you forward. It reminds you why you started, reframes obstacles as training grounds, and strengthens you for the destinations ahead.

Without a map and GPS, you wander. You can move for miles and still not know where you are or where you're going. Purpose is what turns terrain into a true journey—it's what gives your steps direction and your story meaning.

Like all maps, yours will evolve: roads will open, trails will close, and new routes will get redrawn. What felt true at twenty may look different at forty or sixty. That's not failure—it's growth. It means you're still moving, still learning, and still creating your map.

Purpose calls us out of waiting. It says: Don't just dream—Plan A Life You Love and Live it Out Loud Now.

Alignment Check

Fill in the blank—
"I am here to _____."

Don't overthink it. Don't try to make it pretty. Let it be raw, even if it's just a word or phrase. That's your GPS ping marking your current location and reminding you of your direction. Note, there can be more than one answer: I am here to live life fully, to find passion in what I do. I'm here to learn . . . to love, to lead, and to live a life uncommon.

You Are the Cartographer

Some of your terrain has already been charted—the familiar roads of your past, the well-worn trails of habits, the towns and villages built from your experiences. Each mark, each boundary, carries meaning—

sometimes chosen with intention, sometimes inherited by default.

But not everything drawn deserves to stay. Some routes were built on shaky ground. Some markers were never truly yours. In those places, you'll need more than a compass and GPS—you'll need the demolition hammer to break down old stories, clear the rubble of outdated beliefs, and open space for new possibilities.

Beyond the rubble lies open land—vast, uncharted regions waiting for discovery. At first, your map is likely a blend of default and design. But with awareness, you begin to redraw: reinforcing paths that align, rerouting the ones that don't. You build new roads, add shortcuts, merge sections, shift boundaries.

Drifting still charts a map, but it's haphazard—drawn by inheritance and unexamined patterns. That's a map by default. Designing, on the other hand, is cartography driven by intention. Either way, the map will get drawn. That's unavoidable. The question is: Who's holding the pen?

The journey transforms the traveler.

The Path – Contribution (The Mark You Make on the World)

Every step leaves a trace. At first, it's faint, hardly visible in the terrain. But walk it long enough, and it begins to take shape. Walk it with purpose, and it becomes more than your path—it becomes a guide for others.

Contribution is the way your journey touches and shapes those around you as you go. Your contribution is as unique as your journey. No one else can contribute as you can because no one else carries your exact map. Some contributions harm and restrict. Others inspire and encourage. The best ones light the way.

Contribution can happen by default or by design. By default, we pass down unexamined patterns, limiting beliefs, and wounds we never healed. By design, we carve a path of richness—an example worth following.

In my early years of parenting, I often lost my temper, raised my voice, and yes, slammed cabinet doors in passive-aggressive frustration. But as I began to face who I was, who I wanted to become, and the gap in between, I realized it could only be bridged with intentional growth. I can't count the number of times I apologized to my children for my sharp tone and unbecoming behavior. *"I still lose my temper sometimes. If I could have come from my higher self, I would have taken a deep breath, I would have listened, I would have chosen differently... But I'm still rewiring old patterns and learning new ways. You'll have to be patient with me while I grow."*

Their faces would soften every time, and over the years, I saw something shift—they, too, began reaching for better versions of themselves. Every apology, every new choice, became a way of steadying my compass. And once the compass is steady, the next step is inevitable: we begin to look "upward" and outward.

When survival no longer holds us captive and our compass points true, something ancient awakens within us—a hunger to contribute. We long not just to live, but to leave an imprint. To give, to lift, to shape the world in ways that whisper, *I made a difference.*

Conscious contribution shifts us from thinking *"How do I make it through?"* to asking *"How can I make it better for someone else?"* That shift is natural as we self-actualize. It's the sign of a life moving from survival to thrival, from existence to impact.

In the end, the path you walk becomes the path you give.

Alignment Check: The Path You're Leaving

- Complete this sentence: **"My life contributes when I _____."**

- Look at the path you're carving today. Is it one of default—unexamined patterns, habits, and reactions? Or is it one of design—intention, awareness, and choice?
- Ask yourself: *If someone were to follow in my footsteps, where would they end up?*

The Steps – Habits & Daily Choices (How You Move Forward)

A compass may point North, and your GPS may show the way, but neither means anything if you never move your feet. Habits and daily choices are the steps that mobilize your journey.

Some steps are big and bold. Others are small and ordinary. Some are so subtle you may not notice them at the time. Together, they carve the trail beneath your feet and weave your living legacy.

Drift happens one step at a time. Design does too. Every word you speak, every action you take, every response—patient or harsh, thoughtful or careless—plants something in the soil of your life. It might be the overdue conversation that clears the air with a loved one, the email you've avoided, the boundary you need to set, or the risk you've been afraid to take. Over time, these choices accumulate and shape the landscape of your legacy.

Legacy isn't built in grand leaps. It's written in the steady rhythm of daily motion—the step you take when you choose patience instead of frustration, when you wake early to reflect instead of numbing out, when your yes—or your no—aligns with your compass and map. That is how a life on purpose is created: through consistent, intentional steps.

The Alignment Hour – Morning Anchors and Evening Reflections

One of the most powerful ways to take intentional steps is to begin each day by design with an **Alignment Hour**—a sacred pocket of time to steady your compass and sync your GPS. Morning anchors set the tone for how you'll walk through the day:

- **Meditation or Prayer.** Anchor yourself in stillness before stepping into the noise. Visualize who you want to be and how you want to show up in life.

- **Journaling.** Clear your mind, capture insights, connect with your values and desires, and feel appreciation for the richness in your life, and what is going right and well. Celebrate your successes. Write about where you are out of alignment, why, and how you can take steps to align. Also, celebrate where you are aligned.

- **Planning.** Set your priorities for the day. Schedule your "to-dos" and productivity blocks.

- **Affirmations.** Speak words that stabilize and direct you. Pause to reflect on them throughout the day so they can take root in your consciousness.

- **Intention.** Set a guiding intention—your North Star for the day.

- **Expansion.** Feed your mind and spirit with reading, podcasts, or audiobooks.

Your Alignment Hour doesn't have to be exact. Some mornings it may be a full hour—others just 15 minutes. What matters is consistency—checking your bearings before setting out, and making this morning practice a habit.

Evening Check-In – Footprints of the Day

End your day with a **quick check-in**:

- What am I grateful for today?
- What was my favorite part of the day?
- What was the most difficult part of my day? What can I learn from it?
- Where did I stay true to my compass and intention?
- What highlights or wins can I celebrate, however small?
- Where did I drift—and how might I course-correct tomorrow?

This rhythm—anchoring in the morning, reflecting at night—becomes the cadence of design. It helps you unpack the clutter of life. It keeps you steady, present, and intentional.

Each step matters. Each step shapes. Each step writes the story of your life.

Alignment Check: The Steps You're Walking

- Look at the ground you've covered this week. What did you accomplish? Take note of the subtle shifts. Where were you on purpose? How did your choices align with your values? Did you drop seeds of patience, kindness, and truth—or weeds of frustration, distraction, and drift?
- Ask yourself: *What small step can I take today to strengthen the path, align more, or make the journey lighter for the next traveler?*

The Journey Equation – Legacy in Motion

By now, you've seen the pieces of the journey:

- **Compass (Values)** → your True North, the steady orientation.
- **Map (Terrain + GPS and Purpose)** → the lay of the land and the guiding direction that gives meaning to it.

- **Path (Contribution)** → the trail you carve as you walk—the imprint you leave on the hearts of others.
- **Steps (Habits and Behavior)** → the daily motion that carries you forward.

And within each of these tools lie the waypoints that steady you when the terrain gets rough:

- **Values** are your True North.
- **Beliefs** are the lenses that shape what you see.
- **Passions** are the fuel that keep you moving when the road is long.
- **Purpose** is the heart of your GPS, keeping you aligned.

Put them together and you get the equation for a life by design:

Compass + Map + Path + Steps + Waypoints = Legacy in Motion

You are already weaving your legacy. It isn't a destination that waits until you're gone—it's unfolding right now in the way you live, the way you touch others, and the contribution you make each day. Are you on course—or is it time to correct your path?

Legacy is the equation you're solving with every step you take.

Alignment Check: Your Living Eulogy

Write your living eulogy. Not the one spoken at your funeral, but the one spoken now. In the present tense, as if someone is describing you today:

- How do people describe you?
- What do they feel in your presence?
- What trail of contribution are you leaving right now, in the middle of your journey?

Every day is a draft. Every choice edits the story. Every step leaves a mark. What are you creating?

A Living Legacy

As I sit here bringing this chapter to a close, I return to that infamous morning. Coffee in hand. Sunlight shining through the blinds. My youngest, steady at my side. His calm eyes asked a question I could no longer ignore: *What kind of inheritance will you leave us?*

Back then, I didn't have all the answers. I still don't. I only had the ache of knowing something had to change, and I took the first shaky steps on a lifelong journey into self-actualization—a journey of becoming the next best version of myself, over and over again.

When I first stepped into the unknown, I reached for *The Power of Positive Thinking* by Norman Vincent Peale. That book was welcomed and felt like a warm light—it showed me how tangled my thoughts had become and gave me a simple starting place: *Improve your thoughts, Cyndee.* Those words didn't sting; they felt like permission. I underlined. I nodded. I read. I reread. I welcomed every page.

I wish I could say the same for other books. Some confronted me in places I wasn't ready to look.

Victim? Are you saying I'm playing the victim?

That book went flying into the corner, pages splayed, where it sat for three months while I often glared at it for the audacity of speaking truths I wasn't ready to hear.

And humbly, I'll admit—it was the first of many. More than a few books have taken flight across rooms in my house, landing in positions far less dignified than the treasures they truly are.

I didn't realize the map was already there, awaiting my design—values, purpose, passion, contribution. But I had to do the work. I had to sort through the unchallenged beliefs, patterns, and behaviors that had unconsciously shaped my map. I had to discover what was authentically me.

At one point, that meant taking a three-year hiatus from my family of origin—time away to find where I began and where they ended. It wasn't easy. Missing holidays and birthdays left an ache I quietly carried. Family members questioned my choices and, worse, told my two oldest children, *"She doesn't care about you anymore."* I had to sit with them more than once, untangling that lie and reassuring them, *"My love for you has never and will never waver."*

The distance hurt, but it also awakened me. I was the person stepping out of Plato's cave, opening my eyes to possibilities I couldn't see from the station of life in which I was born. Books, seminars, classes, certifications—all widened my horizon, stretched my thinking, and opened doors I hadn't known were there.

And if those big investments expanded my world, it was the daily practice of my Alignment Hour that kept me grounded and moving forward. Every morning: meditation, journaling, planning, affirming my intention, aligning with my compass, reading, listening to audiobooks. That rhythm became the most essential contribution to my journey. It stabilized me in storms, kept me from drifting back into default, and turned theory into transformation. With it, design became daily life.

In the end, I didn't just become the person I wanted my children to become—I became the person I was always meant to be, unknowingly handing them a new kind of family heirloom: a living example of what is possible from a Planned Life—A Life by Design.

When I think about legacy now, I can't help but return to my mom. She raised four kids in a world that rarely gave women a seat at the table, and yet she found her way and made her mark. She was philanthropic to her core, a force to be reckoned with when she caught a vision of good. That was part of her living legacy, reminding me that even in the most ordinary of days, contribution ripples outward.

And she was her father's daughter. My grandfather was also deeply philanthropic—one of the founders of the San Leandro Boys Club, just one of many projects he poured himself into, each an investment in something bigger than himself. In my own way, I'm continuing the thread they began. Their examples whisper through every step I take to design a life on purpose, proving that what we live becomes what we leave.

And now, dear reader, back to you . . . the wave reaches your shore—what ripple will your life set in motion?

This is my invitation to you: Stop drifting. Start designing. And then—start driving. You don't have to have the entire map; you just need to take the first steps and commit to the journey. The way will show you the way. Be patient with yourself. Be forgiving. It's not a straight arrow path. It will be filled with "writer's block moments," "shitty first drafts," and lots of red marks. But in the end, it is a journey every soul craves—the journey toward self, purpose, contribution, and impact.

A life by design isn't static. It's not just a plan on paper. It's a living, breathing legacy in motion—fueled by your drive.

Don't wait to be remembered. **Plan a Life You Love and Live it Out Loud Now.**

JOIN THE MOVEMENT!
#BAUW

Becoming An Unstoppable Woman
With She Rises Studios

She Rises Studios was founded by Hanna Olivas and Adriana Luna Carlos, the mother-daughter duo, in mid-2020 as they saw a need to help empower women worldwide. They are the podcast hosts of the *She Rises Studios Podcast* and Amazon best-selling authors and motivational speakers who travel the world. Hanna and Adriana are the movement creators of #BAUW - Becoming An Unstoppable Woman: The movement has been created to universally impact women of all ages, at whatever stage of life, to overcome insecurities, and adversities, and develop an unstoppable mindset. She Rises Studios educates, celebrates, and empowers women globally.

Looking to Join Us in our Next Anthology or Publish YOUR Own?

She Rises Studios Publishing offers full-service publishing, marketing, book tour, and campaign services. For more information, contact info@sherisesstudios.com

We are always looking for women who want to share their stories and expertise and feature their businesses on our podcasts, in our books, and in our magazines.

SEE WHAT WE DO

OUR PODCAST

OUR BOOKS

OUR SERVICES

Be featured in the Becoming An Unstoppable Woman magazine, published in 13 countries and sold in all major retailers. Get the visibility you need to LEVEL UP in your business!

Have your own TV show streamed across major platforms like Roku TV, Amazon Fire Stick, Apple TV and more!

Learn to leverage your expertise. Build your online presence and grow your audience with FENIX TV.
https://fenixtv.sherisesstudios.com/

Visit www.SheRisesStudios.com to see how YOU can join the #BAUW movement and help your community to achieve the UNSTOPPABLE mindset.

Have you checked out the *She Rises Studios Podcast?*

Find us on all MAJOR platforms: Spotify, IHeartRadio, Apple Podcasts, Google Podcasts, etc.

Looking to become a sponsor or build a partnership?

Email us at info@sherisesstudios.com

www.ingramcontent.com/pod-product-compliance
Lightning Source LLC
Chambersburg PA
CBHW061702120626
46550CB00003B/1055